HIRED TONGUE

Published by - Spines
ISBN: 979-8-89569-082-6

Hired Tongue

The Talk Radio Adventures of
The Ed Tyll Show

Ed Tyll

FOREWORD

When Edward Tyll first walked into my office, I knew he was destined for greatness. His enthusiasm was infectious, his energy boundless, and his intellectual skills were razor-sharp. But what truly set him apart was his voice - a unique, captivating sound that commanded attention and sparked curiosity.

From the moment I heard him speak, I knew he was a natural-born broadcaster. He had a gift for spontaneous verbal expression, a talent for weaving words into captivating stories that could make you laugh, cry, and think deeply about the world around you.

Ed was a pathfinder, a pioneer in the world of talk radio. He wasn't afraid to push boundaries, to challenge conventional wisdom, and to tackle controversial topics with humor and intelligence. He was a breath of fresh air in a stale industry, a voice that resonated with listeners who were tired of the same old talking points and predictable formats.

Over the years, I watched with pride as Ed's career soared. He became a household name, a beloved figure in the communities he served, and a true icon of talk radio. But through it all, he never lost his passion, his energy, or his unique voice.

This book is a testament to Ed's remarkable journey, a collection of stories that capture the highs and lows, the triumphs and challenges, of a life dedicated to the art of broadcasting. It's a must-read for anyone who loves radio, who appreciates the power of the spoken word, and who believes in the importance of following your dreams.

So sit back, relax, and enjoy the ride. Ed Tyll is about to take you on a wild and unforgettable adventure through the world of talk radio.

Everett Bigglesworth

Chapter 1

Blackout Bonanza

In a grid-locked horn honking intersection on New York City's midtown west side, where dreams shimmer like stars in the night sky, I embarked on a thrilling adventure to become a talk radio show host.

Picture me: a charismatic chap with a voice smoother than velvet and a wit sharper than a tack. With a microphone in a studio and a twinkle in my eye, I was ready to unleash hilarity upon the airwaves.

My show, aptly titled "The Ed Tyll Show," quickly gained a cult following. People from all walks of life tuned in to hear my unique blend of humor, wit, and unabashed absurdity. Each episode was a rollercoaster ride of laughter and unexpected twists that left listeners both entertained and bewildered.

One unforgettable segment involved a caller who claimed to have invented a device that could translate animal languages. Intrigued and slightly skeptical, I engaged in a hilarious conversation with a parrot named Polly, who shared her surprisingly sophisticated views on politics and pop culture. The audience couldn't stop chuckling as I tried to maintain a straight face while Polly critiqued the latest fashion trends.

Another time, I conducted a live experiment where I challenged listeners to identify various household objects blindfolded while blindfolded. The results were nothing short of comical. From mistaking a vacuum cleaner for a musical instrument to labeling a frying pan as a UFO, the participants' wild guesses had me and the audience in stitches.

But it wasn't all fun and games. I also had the privilege of hosting interviews with some of the most eccentric characters imaginable. There was the self-proclaimed time traveler who claimed to have witnessed the construction of the pyramids, a conspiracy theorist who believed Elvis Presley was still alive and hiding in the Bermuda Triangle, and even a professional mermaid who shared her insights on underwater etiquette. Each interview was a testament to the boundless creativity and imagination of my listeners.

Of course, no talk radio show is without its technical difficulties. One particularly memorable incident involved a sudden power outage during a live broadcast. Undeterred, I continued my show in the darkness, relying solely on my wit and the sound of my own laughter. The audience loved it, and the episode became known as the "Blackout Bonanza."

As my show's popularity grew, so did my celebrity status. I was invited to star in commercials, appear on television programs, and even write a self-help book titled "How to Talk Your Way Out of Anything." The book became an instant bestseller, thanks to its hilarious anecdotes and unconventional advice on navigating life's awkward situations.

But amidst the laughter and accolades, I remained grounded. I never forgot my humble beginnings as a small-town boy with big dreams. And so, every day, I would go on the air, eager to share my brand of humor with the world, hoping to bring joy to even the darkest of days.

And so, my journey as a talk radio show host continued, filled with countless hilarious moments, unforgettable characters, and the unwavering support of my loyal listeners. Through it all, I never lost sight of my mission: to make people laugh and to remind them that even in the midst of life's absurdities, there's always room for a good chuckle.

It all began for me during a huge snow storm.

I was born on a snowy night in New York City's northern borough, The Bronx. The blizzard was so bad that my father had to dig our car out of the snow just to get my mother to the hospital. When I finally arrived, the doctor couldn't help but chuckle at the sight of my tiny red face peeking out from beneath a blanket of snow.

"Well, it looks like we have a little snow bunny on our hands!" he exclaimed.

As the snow continued to fall outside, I was swaddled in a cozy blanket and placed in my mother's arms. She looked down at me with love and amusement, and I couldn't help but feel like the luckiest baby in the world to be born into such a magical winter wonderland.

But my snowy entrance into the world didn't end there. As my parents drove me home from the hospital, the snow started to come down even harder. The roads were treacherous, and my father had to drive extra carefully. At one point, we even got stuck in a snowdrift and had to be rescued by a passing plow truck.

Despite the challenges, my parents were in high spirits. They couldn't stop talking about how happy they were to have me in their lives. And as I looked out the window at the snow-covered streets, I felt a sense of peace and contentment that I had never experienced before.

That night, as I slept soundly in my crib, the snow continued to fall outside. It was as if the entire city was celebrating my arrival. And as the sun rose the next morning, I woke up to a world transformed into a winter wonderland. The snow sparkled like diamonds, and the trees were covered in a thick layer of white.

My parents bundled me up in warm clothes and took me outside to see the snow for the first time. I was amazed by its beauty and couldn't stop reaching out to touch it. As I played in the snow, I felt a connection to nature that I had never felt before.

And so, my journey in this world began on a snowy night in New York City. It was a magical start to a life filled with love, laughter, and adventure. And every time it snows, I can't help but smile and remember the day I was born—the day the snow bunny arrived.

Chapter 2

First Show Fiasco

The first time I hosted a beachside radio show, I was determined to make a splash. I envisioned myself as a suave and witty host, entertaining sunbathers with my charming banter and hilarious anecdotes. Little did I know that the ocean had other plans for me.

As I arrived at the beach, I was greeted by a stunning view of the coastline. Waves were crashing against the golden sand, and the seagulls were soaring overhead. I set up my equipment, eager to get started. The sun was shining brightly, and the atmosphere was perfect for a day of fun and laughter.

I kicked off the show with a cheerful greeting. I had some upbeat music to play and a few jokes to share, hoping to warm up the crowd. So far, everything was going swimmingly.

But then, disaster struck. As I was in the middle of a hilarious story about a talking crab, a rogue wave suddenly crashed over my equipment, drenching me from head to toe. My headphones filled with water, and my microphone started to emit a series of earsplitting squelches.

I stood there, soaked to the bone, trying to maintain my composure as the audience erupted into laughter. I couldn't help but join in on the fun, realizing that this was one of those moments you just had to embrace.

With the help of a few beachgoers, I managed to salvage my equipment and continue the show. I improvised a segment called "Wet and Wild Radio," where I shared stories of other unfortunate beachside mishaps and invited listeners to call in with their own tales of woe.

To my surprise, the audience loved it. They were cheering me on, offering me towels, and even sharing their sunscreen to help me dry off. I realized that sometimes, the best radio shows are the ones that go off the rails in the most unexpected ways.

From that day on, I became known as the "Wet and Wild Radio Guy." I continued to host beachside radio shows, but I always made sure to keep a close eye on the ocean, just in case it decided to play another prank on me.

And so, my first beachside radio show went down in history as a hilarious disaster that turned into an unforgettable experience. It taught me that even when things go wrong, you can always find a way to laugh it off and turn it into a memorable moment for both yourself and your audience.

In the end, I learned that the most important thing about hosting a beachside radio show is to be prepared for anything. You never know when a rogue wave might come crashing down on you, but if you can embrace the chaos and find a way to make it entertaining, you'll have a show that people will never forget.

Early Days

Chapter 3

Not Bigglesworthy

My boss, Mr. Bigglesworth, was a strict and serious man. He had a reputation for being humorless and demanding, and I had always been careful to avoid his wrath. That is, until the day I accidentally upset him with my talk radio show.

It was a slow news day, and I was running out of ideas for my show. In a moment of desperation, I decided to do a segment on the funniest office pranks I had ever witnessed. I shared a few harmless anecdotes about my colleagues, making sure to change their names and some details to protect their identities.

Little did I know, Mr. Bigglesworth was listening.

The next day, he summoned me to his office. As I entered, I could see the storm clouds gathering on his face.

"Mr. Tyll," he began, his voice cold and menacing, "I understand you've been using your talk radio show to make fun of your colleagues."

I was caught off guard. "But sir, I changed their names and some details. They're not identifiable," I protested.

"That's not the point," he snapped. "You're making our company look unprofessional. I don't want our employees to think we're a joke."

I tried to explain that my intentions were harmless and that I was just trying to entertain my listeners, but Mr. Bigglesworth was having none of it.

"You're suspended from the radio show until further notice," he declared. "And consider yourself lucky I'm not firing you."

I left his office feeling dejected and defeated. I had never meant to upset Mr. Bigglesworth or embarrass the company. I just wanted to make people laugh.

A few days later, I was surprised to receive a call from Mr. Bigglesworth. He apologized for overreacting and admitted that he had been under a lot of stress lately. He reinstated me to the radio show and even encouraged me to continue doing my prank segments, as long as I was more careful about protecting my colleagues' identities.

I learned a valuable lesson that day: when it comes to humor, it's always best to err on the side of caution, especially when your boss is known for having a short fuse.

CHAPTER 4

DINNER DEBACLE

It was a Friday night, and I was supposed to be enjoying a romantic dinner with my girlfriend, Sarah. But instead, I found myself trapped in the radio station, hosting my talk show.

It all started when I got a call from my boss, Mr. Bigglesworth.

"I know it's your night off, but we have a special guest who canceled at the last minute," he said. "I need you to come in and fill in."

I groaned. I had been looking forward to my date with Sarah all week, but I knew I couldn't say no to Mr. Bigglesworth.

"Okay, I'll be there," I sighed.

As I drove to the station, I tried to think of a way to make it up to Sarah. Maybe I could take her out to dinner the following night.

When I arrived at the station, I was greeted by a frantic producer.

"The guest canceled five minutes ago," she said. "We don't have a backup, and we're live in ten minutes."

I panicked. I had never hosted a show without a guest before.

"Don't worry," I said, trying to sound confident. "I'll figure something out."

I ran into the studio and grabbed the microphone.

"Ladies and gentlemen," I said, "welcome to the show. Tonight, we're going to be talking about..."

I trailed off, my mind blank. I had no idea what to talk about.

Then, I remembered a story about a time when I accidentally ate a live microphone during a live broadcast. I figured, what the heck, I might as well share it.

I started telling the story, and to my surprise, the audience loved it. They were laughing and calling in with their own stories about embarrassing moments.

By the time the show was over, I had completely forgotten about my date with Sarah. I was so caught up in the excitement of the show that I didn't even realize how late it was.

When I finally got home, Sarah was asleep. I crept into bed and fell asleep, exhausted but happy.

The next morning, I woke up to the sound of Sarah shaking me awake.

"What time do you call this?" she asked, groggy.

I smiled. "I had a little bit of a mishap at work," I said.

I told her about the canceled guest and the impromptu show. She laughed and shook her head.

"Only you," she said. "But I'm glad you had fun."

I smiled. "Me too," I said. "And I'm sorry I missed our date. How about we try again tonight?"

Sarah smiled. "Sounds good to me," she said.

And so, after a night of unexpected radio hijinks, I finally made it to my dinner date with Sarah. And this time, nothing stood in our way.

UPI
United Press International
Broadcasters of Florida
1985
AWARDS OF EXCELLENCE
EDWARD F. TYLL
WPBR, Palm Beach
First Place
Coverage of an Extraordinary Event

The UPI

Chapter 5

Storm Work

Working at a radio station located right on the beach in Florida was a dream come true, until a hurricane came barreling towards us. As the winds picked up and the rain started coming down sideways, I found myself broadcasting live updates to our listeners, while simultaneously trying to keep my equipment from being swept away by the storm surge.

The power flickered on and off, and the sound of the wind howling outside was so loud that I could barely hear myself think. But the show must go on, as they say, and I was determined to keep our listeners informed and entertained, even if it meant risking life and limb.

At one point, a particularly strong gust of wind blew open the studio door, sending papers and equipment flying everywhere. I had to dive under the desk to avoid being hit by a rogue microphone stand. When I emerged, soaked and disheveled, I couldn't help but laugh at the absurdity of the situation.

As the hurricane raged on, I continued to broadcast updates, sharing stories of survival and resilience from our listeners who were hunkered down in their homes. We even had a call from a woman who was riding out the storm in her bathtub with her pet parrot, who was apparently quite unfazed by the whole ordeal.

Finally, after what seemed like an eternity, the hurricane passed, leaving behind a trail of destruction. But the radio station was still standing, and I was still on the air, albeit a little worse for wear.

As I looked out the window at the battered coastline, I couldn't help but feel a sense of pride in what we had accomplished. We had stayed on the air throughout the storm, providing a vital service to our community. And we had done it with a healthy dose of humor and good old-fashioned grit.

Happy Word Warrior

CHAPTER 6

BEACH GIRL

After a long day of on-air antics and listener calls, I decided to take a walk on the beach behind the station to relax. The sun was setting, casting a warm glow over the sand and waves. As I strolled along the shoreline, I noticed a figure sitting on a beach towel, reading a book.

Intrigued, I decided to strike up a conversation. "Nice evening, isn't it?" I offered, trying to sound casual and not too much like a radio announcer.

Her eyes sparkled with amusement as she looked up from her book. "It is," she replied, her voice as smooth as the ocean breeze. "And it's even better now."

We chatted for a while, and I learned her name was Maya. She was visiting from out of town and had been drawn to the beach by the sound of my show drifting through the open window of her hotel room. She confessed she had found my stories and jokes hilarious, especially the one about the talking crab.

Flattered and emboldened, I invited her to join me for a drink at a nearby beachside bar. As we sipped our margaritas and watched the stars come out, I realized I was enjoying her company even more than the stunning sunset.

Maya was not only beautiful but also intelligent, witty, and had a laugh that made my heart skip a beat. We talked for hours, sharing stories, dreams, and our mutual love for the beach.

As the night drew to a close, I knew I didn't want it to end. I walked her back to her hotel, and under the soft glow of the moonlight, we shared a kiss that was as sweet and salty as the ocean air.

From that day on, Maya became a regular listener of my show, and we continued to meet for walks on the beach and margaritas at the bar. And every time I see her, I'm reminded that sometimes, the best things in life happen when you least expect them, like stumbling upon a beautiful girl while taking a walk on the beach after a long day at work.

Chapter 7

Late Panic

Panic sets in like a swarm of angry bees. My show starts in 30 minutes, and I'm miles away from the nearest town. To make matters worse, my phone battery is at a measly 2%. I frantically scan the desolate landscape, hoping to spot a passing car, but it seems like I'm the only living soul on this forsaken stretch of road.

Just when I'm about to lose all hope, a rusty old pickup truck appears on the horizon. It rattles to a stop beside me, and the driver, a grizzled old farmer with a mischievous twinkle in his eye, steps out. He takes one look at my predicament and tosses me a rope.

"Hold on tight, city slicker," he says with a grin.

With my car in tow, we embark on a bumpy ride down the highway. I'm bouncing around in the backseat like a ragdoll, desperately trying to hold on to my notes and my dignity.

Finally, we arrive at the radio station with minutes to spare. I burst through the door, disheveled and out of breath, just as the producer is about to call the police to report me missing.

"You're late!" she exclaims, a mixture of relief and exasperation in her voice.

I stumble into the studio and take my seat behind the microphone. My heart is pounding, my clothes are covered in dust, and I'm pretty sure I still have rope burns on my hands.

But as soon as the "On Air" light flicks on, I plaster a smile on my face and launch into my show. I regale my listeners with the hilarious tale of my unexpected detour, complete with sound effects and dramatic reenactments.

The audience loves it. They're calling in with their own stories of car troubles and near-misses. My producer is laughing so hard she's crying.

And me? I'm just grateful to be alive, on the air, and sharing my ridiculous misadventures with the world. Because let's face it, even the most disastrous car breakdown can become a hilarious story with the right attitude and a little bit of comedic timing.

Presidential Pundit

CHAPTER 8

ON SCENE LIVE

It was a typical evening in South Florida, the kind where the humidity clung to you like a wet blanket and the air was thick with the scent of coconut-scented sunscreen. I had just finished a grueling shift at the radio station, where I was hosting my talk show, "The Ed Tyll Show." My brain was buzzing with the day's topics, and I was eager to get home, kick off my shoes, and relax with a cold drink.

As I drove down the palm-lined streets, my police scanner crackled to life. A robbery is underway at a local Eckerd's drugstore, just a few blocks from my apartment. My reporter instincts kicked in, and I made a split-second decision. I wasn't going home yet.

I swung my car and headed to the scene. As I got closer, I could see flashing lights and a growing crowd of onlookers. Police cars surrounded the store, their sirens silent but their lights casting an eerie glow over the scene.

I parked my car a safe distance away and grabbed my trusty tape recorder. I knew I had to get the scoop, but I also knew that getting too close to the action could be dangerous. So, I did what any resourceful reporter would do: I found a payphone.

Thankfully, I had a pocketful of quarters, a relic from my childhood days of calling my friends on landlines. I dialed the station's number and was immediately patched through to the newsroom.

"Ed Tyll here, live on the scene," I announced, trying to sound as professional as possible despite the fact that I was standing in a dimly lit phone booth, surrounded by buzzing mosquitoes.

For the next four hours, I became the eyes and ears of our listeners. I described the scene in detail, relaying information from police officers, witnesses, and even the occasional bystander who was eager to share their two cents.

I interviewed a woman who had been inside the store when the robbery began. She described the fear and panic that had gripped everyone as the robber, armed with a gun, herded them into a back room. Her voice trembled as she recounted how she had prayed for her life and the lives of her coworkers.

I spoke to a policeman who was part of the team negotiating with the robber. He explained the delicate balance they had to strike between ensuring the safety of the hostages and apprehending the suspect. His calm and measured demeanor was reassuring, but I could sense the tension in his voice.

As the hours dragged on, the crowd of onlookers grew larger. People were drawn to the drama unfolding before them, their faces illuminated by the flashing lights of the police cars. Some were offering words of encouragement to the officers, while others were speculating about the robber's motives and the fate of the hostages.

I continued to report on the situation, my voice becoming hoarse from the constant talking. I was exhausted, hungry, and starting to feel the effects of the mosquito bites, but I knew I couldn't stop. This was a story that mattered to our community, and I was determined to see it through.

Finally, after what seemed like an eternity, the standoff ended. The robber surrendered peacefully, and the hostages were released unharmed. A cheer erupted from the crowd as the police led the suspect away in handcuffs.

I wrapped up my report, thanking the listeners for their patience and expressing my relief that the situation had been resolved without bloodshed. As I hung up the phone, I realized that my arm was sore from holding the receiver for so long.

I walked back to my car, feeling a mixture of exhaustion and exhilaration. I had just witnessed a major news event unfold before my eyes, and I had played a small but important role in keeping our listeners informed.

As I drove home, I couldn't help but smile. It wasn't the relaxing evening I had planned, but it was certainly one I would never forget. And as I drifted off to sleep that night, I dreamed of phone booths, police scanners, and the thrill of chasing the next big story.

Chapter 9

Near Break Up

Bringing my girlfriend, Sarah, to the annual National Association of Broadcasters (NAB) convention in Las Vegas seemed like a brilliant idea at first. She'd get to experience the glitz and glamor of Sin City, while I'd catch up with old friends, make new connections, and maybe even score a few freebies from the tech vendors. What could possibly go wrong?

Plenty, as it turns out.

The first sign of trouble appeared when we checked into our hotel room. Sarah had envisioned a luxurious suite with a view of the Strip, but due to a mix-up with our reservation, we ended up in a cramped room overlooking the parking lot. Not exactly the romantic getaway she had imagined.

Things got worse at the convention itself. While I was busy schmoozing with fellow radio personalities and geeking out over the latest broadcasting equipment, Sarah was left to wander the exhibit hall alone, bored and increasingly irritated.

"Why did you even bring me here if you were just going to ignore me?" she asked, her voice rising above the din of the crowd.

I tried to explain that the NAB was a networking event, and that I needed to make the most of it for my career. But Sarah wasn't having it.

"Networking? More like Nerd-working!" she retorted, rolling her eyes.

To make matters worse, I kept bumping into old flames and former colleagues, all of whom seemed to be having a much better time than Sarah. There was the vivacious morning show host from Miami, the witty sports commentator from Chicago, and even my ex-girlfriend, the sultry news anchor from New York.

Sarah's patience finally snapped when I introduced her to my old buddy, the infamous shock jock known for his outrageous on-air stunts.

"So, you're the one who's been keeping Ed from spending time with me," she said, her tone dripping with sarcasm.

The shock jock, never one to shy away from controversy, grinned mischievously. "Guilty as charged, sweetheart. But don't worry, I'll make it up to you. How about a round of shots at the bar?"

Before I could intervene, Sarah had grabbed the shock jock's arm and was dragging him towards the nearest watering hole. I watched in horror as they disappeared into the crowd, leaving me to fend for myself.

For the rest of the convention, I was caught in a tug-of-war between my professional obligations and my personal life. I tried to appease Sarah by taking her to fancy dinners and shows, but she remained aloof and resentful.

"I feel like I'm just an accessory to your career," she complained. "You don't really care about me, do you?"

I tried to reassure her that I did care, but deep down, I knew she had a point. I had been so focused on my own ambitions that I had neglected her needs.

The final straw came on the convention's final night. We were at a swanky after-party, surrounded by industry bigwigs and celebrities. Sarah, looking stunning in a red dress, was finally starting to enjoy herself. But then, I got pulled aside by a group of radio executives who wanted to discuss a potential syndication deal for my show.

I apologized to Sarah, promising to be back in a few minutes. But as the conversation dragged on, I lost track of time. When I finally returned to the party, Sarah was nowhere to be found.

I frantically searched the venue, but she was gone. I called her phone, but it went straight to voicemail. I was starting to panic.

Finally, I found her sitting alone at a blackjack table, nursing a drink and looking utterly miserable.

"Where were you?" she asked, her voice barely audible.

I explained the meeting, but she cut me.

"I don't want to hear it," she said, her eyes filled with tears. "I'm going back to the hotel."

As I watched her leave, I realized I had made a huge mistake. I had brought her to the NAB thinking it would be a fun and exciting experience. Instead, I had made her feel neglected and unimportant.

As Sarah disappeared into the crowd with the shock jock, a wave of conflicting emotions washed over me. Part of me was relieved to have a moment to myself, to regroup and strategize my next move at the convention. Another part of me was worried about Sarah, knowing her penchant for getting carried away after a few drinks. But mostly, I was just curious. What on earth were they talking about? Was she grilling him about my past, or was she actually enjoying his company?

I decided to give them some space and headed back to the exhibit hall, hoping to salvage what was left of my professional reputation. As I wandered through the booths, I couldn't help but feel a pang of guilt. Sarah had been right – I had been neglecting her, caught up in the excitement of the convention and the thrill of reconnecting with old friends.

A few hours later, I received a text message from Sarah: "Meet us at the karaoke bar in 10 minutes. You're up next."

I groaned. Karaoke was not my forte, and the thought of singing in front of a crowd of strangers, especially after a few drinks, filled me with dread. But I knew I couldn't back out now. Sarah would never let me hear the end of it.

I arrived at the karaoke bar to find Sarah and the shock jock already on stage, belting out a duet of "Don't Stop Believin'" with gusto. The crowd was cheering them on, and even the notoriously stoic bartender was tapping his foot to the beat.

As their song ended, Sarah spotted me and waved me over. "Get up here, Ed!" she shouted, her face flushed with excitement. "It's your turn!"

I reluctantly took the stage, my heart pounding in my chest. The shock jock handed me a microphone and whispered, "Don't worry, buddy. Just pick a song you know and let it rip."

I scanned the song list, my eyes landing on "Bohemian Rhapsody" by Queen. It was a challenging song, but I knew every word by heart. I took a deep breath and started singing.

At first, my voice was shaky and hesitant, but as I got into the groove, I started to feel more confident. I hit the high notes, nailed the harmonies, and even threw in a few air guitar moves for good measure. The crowd went wild, and Sarah was beaming with pride.

By the end of the song, I was sweating profusely and my throat was sore, but I had never felt so alive. I had conquered my fear of karaoke, and I had done it in front of the woman I loved and a room full of strangers.

As I stepped off the stage, Sarah threw her arms around me and kissed me passionately. "That was amazing!" she exclaimed. "I knew you had it in you."

I grinned sheepishly. "Thanks," I said. "I guess I just needed a little liquid courage and a push from the shock jock."

From that moment on, the NAB convention took on a whole new meaning for me. It wasn't just networking and career advancement anymore. It was about having fun, letting loose, and sharing unforgettable experiences with the people who mattered most to me.

And as for Sarah and the shock jock, they became unlikely friends, bonding over their shared love of karaoke and their ability to bring out the wild side in me. And every time we hear "Bohemian

Rhapsody" on the radio, we can't help but laugh and remember the night I almost lost my voice, but found my groove.

Broadcast Journalist

CHAPTER 10

BREAKING NEWS

It was a quiet Wednesday afternoon at the radio station. The kind of afternoon where the only sound was the gentle hum of the air conditioner and the occasional ticking of the clock on the wall. I was the sole soul left in the newsroom, everyone else having gone out for a long lunch or errands. I was happily typing away at a rather mundane story about a local pie-eating contest when suddenly, the newsroom phone erupted in a shrill ring.

"With your Afternoon News, this is Ed Tyll reporting," I answered, trying to sound professional although I was half-expecting a telemarketer.

"Ed, thank heavens you're there!" It was the station manager, his voice laced with panic. "Turn on the TV, channel 7, now!"

Before I could even ask what was happening, he hung up. With a growing sense of dread, I switched on the small TV in the corner of the newsroom. The screen flickered to life, revealing a scene of utter chaos. A massive earthquake had struck downtown, causing buildings to crumble and sending people fleeing in terror.

My heart pounded in my chest as I realized the gravity of the situation. This was huge news, and I was the only reporter on hand to cover it. The adrenaline kicked in, and I went into autopilot, grabbing my microphone and headphones.

"Ladies and gentlemen," I announced, my voice shaking slightly, "we are coming to you live with breaking news. A major earthquake has just struck downtown..."

For the next several hours, I was a one-man news team. I juggled phone calls from frantic witnesses, monitored the police scanner for updates, and scrambled to write coherent news bulletins. I even managed to get a live phone interview with a woman who had been trapped in an elevator during the quake. Her voice was shaky, but she bravely recounted her ordeal, adding a human touch to the unfolding disaster.

As the hours passed, the newsroom became a whirlwind of activity. Phones were ringing off the hook, the teletype machine was spitting out updates, and I was frantically typing away at my computer, trying to keep up with the flood of information.

Despite the chaos, I couldn't help but feel a sense of exhilaration. This was what I had always dreamed of: being in the thick of the action, reporting on a major news event as it unfolded. And even though I was flying by the seat of my pants, I was determined to do my best to keep our listeners informed.

As the sun began to set, the earthquake's aftermath became clearer. The damage was extensive, but thankfully, there were no reports of fatalities. As the adrenaline wore off, exhaustion set in. I could barely keep my eyes open, but I knew I had to stay on air until the late-night crew arrived.

Finally, around midnight, my replacement walked through the door. I handed him the microphone, gave him a quick rundown of the situation, and stumbled out of the newsroom, feeling like I had just run a marathon.

As I drove home, I couldn't help but reflect on the day's events. It had been a baptism by fire, but I had come through it, and I had done it alone. I had proven to myself, and to my colleagues, that I could handle even the most challenging news stories.

And as I drifted off to sleep that night, I dreamed of earthquakes, breaking news, and the thrill of being the first to report the story.

Breaking News

Chapter 11

On Air Ambush

The early days of my talk radio career were a whirlwind of excitement, caffeine-fueled nights, and the occasional on-air blunder. As the producer of "The Evening Review Show," I was responsible for booking guests, crafting engaging topics, and ensuring the host didn't accidentally insult any major politicians or celebrities. It was a high-pressure job, but I loved every minute.

Our show was a unique blend of news, entertainment, and cultural commentary, and we had a loyal following of listeners who tuned in every night to hear our take on the day's events. We tackled everything from politics and current affairs to the latest celebrity gossip and pop culture trends.

But then, the station manager decided to shake things up. He announced that "The Evening Review Show" would be rebranded as an all-sports talk show, catering to the city's die-hard sports fans. This was a major departure from our established format, and none of us were particularly thrilled about the change.

Despite our reservations, we tried to make the best of it. We booked interviews with local athletes, debated the merits of various sports teams, and even attempted to learn the rules of cricket (which, for the record, is a baffling and utterly confusing sport).

However, it quickly became apparent that our hearts weren't in it. Our attempts at sports commentary were often awkward and stilted, and our listeners weren't impressed. The ratings plummeted, and the station manager was furious.

One fateful evening, after a particularly disastrous show where we accidentally referred to the Super Bowl as the "Superb Owl," the ax fell. We were all fired, effective immediately.

Dejected and unemployed, we decided to drown our sorrows at the nearest bar. As we sat there, nursing our beers and lamenting the end of an era, a strange thing happened. We started to laugh.

We laughed about the absurd sports segments we had been forced to do, the ridiculous guests we had interviewed, and the countless on-air blunders we had made. We laughed until our sides ached and tears streamed down our faces.

At that moment, I realized that even though our show had been canceled, we had shared something special. We had been a team, a family, and we had created something that, for a brief moment in time, had brought joy and laughter to our listeners.

And so, we raised our glasses to "The Evening Review Show," to the memories we had made, and to the future, whatever it might hold. As we stumbled out of the bar that night, arm in arm and still chuckling, I knew that even though we were no longer on the air, the spirit of our show would live on in our hearts.

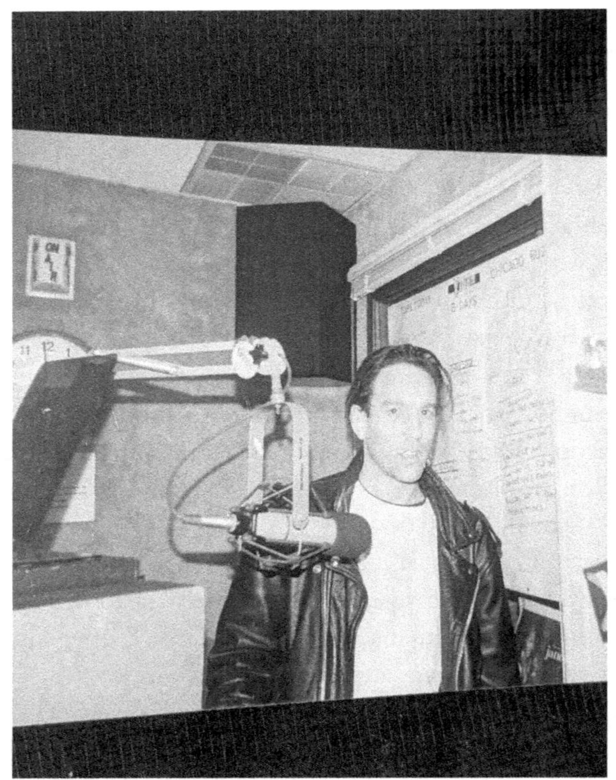

Hot Talker

CHAPTER 12

THE FLIGHT ATTENDANT

The ink on my contract with Baltimore's legendary talk radio station was barely dry when I decided to celebrate my big break with a night on the town. After packing my bags and bidding farewell to my cramped New York apartment, I boarded a flight to Charm City, my heart pounding with a mixture of excitement and trepidation.

As fate would have it, the flight attendant assigned to my row was a vision in blue: tall, slender, with a captivating smile that could melt even the most hardened cynic's heart. Her name tag read "Tiffany," and her witty banter and impeccable service made the otherwise mundane flight a delightful experience.

We chatted about everything from our favorite travel destinations to our shared love of live music. By the time the plane touched down in Baltimore, I was smitten. And it seemed the feeling was mutual.

"So, what brings you to Baltimore?" Tiffany asked as I gathered my belongings.

"I'm starting a new job as a talk radio host," I replied, trying to sound nonchalant despite the butterflies fluttering in my stomach.

"Wow, that's impressive," she said, her eyes widening with admiration. "Maybe I'll have to tune in."

"You definitely should," I said with a grin. "And if you're ever free on a Friday night, there's a great dance club downtown..."

Tiffany laughed. "Smooth, Ed. But I like it. Here's my number. Give me a call sometime."

As I stepped off the plane and into the bustling terminal, I couldn't help but feel like I had just won the lottery. Not only had I landed my dream job, but I had also met a beautiful and intriguing woman who seemed genuinely interested in me.

That night, after checking into my hotel and freshening up, I decided to take Tiffany up on her offer. I dialed her number, and a few minutes later, we were meeting at the trendy dance club she had recommended.

The music was loud, the lights were flashing, and the dance floor was packed with gyrating bodies. Tiffany, wearing a slinky black dress that hugged her curves in all the right places, was a natural on the dance floor. She moved with grace and confidence, her long hair swirling around her like a dark halo.

I, on the other hand, was a bit more awkward. My dance moves were more reminiscent of a spastic marionette than a suave Latin lover. But Tiffany didn't seem to mind. She laughed at my clumsy attempts to keep up with her, and her infectious energy soon had me moving and grooving with abandon.

We danced for hours, lost in each other's music and company. As the night wore on, the chemistry between us became undeniable. We shared stolen glances, whispered jokes, and our bodies moved closer and closer together.

When the club closed, we were both breathless and exhilarated. We walked out into the cool night air, hand in hand, and shared a kiss that was as sweet and intoxicating as the cocktails we had been sipping.

In the days that followed, Tiffany and I became inseparable. We explored Baltimore together, discovering its hidden gems and quirky charms. We sampled crab cakes at waterfront restaurants, cheered on the Orioles at Camden Yards, and danced the night away at countless clubs and bars.

As my first show approached, I was filled with a newfound sense of confidence. I knew that no matter how challenging the job might be, I had Tiffany by my side to support and encourage me.

So my new life in Baltimore began with a bang. I had a dream job, a beautiful girlfriend, and a city full of possibilities waiting to be explored. It was the start of a thrilling adventure, and I couldn't wait to see where it would take me.

But format changes abound. It was contract buyout time.

Quickly the phone rang from Albany. In 72 hours I was setting up an apartment in Menands, starting my new show in the Capitol District with an article featuring my arrival on the front page of the local magazine.

Hosting the morning talk show in Albany, New York, meant being at the station by 4 a.m., an ungodly hour that even roosters scoffed at. But the thrill of being the voice that woke up the city, that blend of information and humor to kick start their day, made it worthwhile. Until the infamous blizzard of '93 decided to test my dedication.

It started innocently enough, a few flurries during my late-night dinner. By the time I hit the road, it was a full-blown snowpocalypse. The roads were quickly disappearing under a thick white blanket, and my trusty old Pontiac Fiero was struggling to stay on course.

Halfway to the station, the inevitable happened. My car sputtered, coughed, and died, leaving me stranded on a deserted stretch of highway. The wind howled like a banshee, the snow piled up around my car, and I could feel the cold seeping into my bones.

I tried calling the station, but my phone was as dead as my car. I considered walking, but the blizzard was so thick I could barely see my own hand in front of my face. Hypothermia was starting to set in, and I was seriously considering building a snowman and curling up inside it for warmth.

Just when I thought I was a goner, a pair of headlights appeared through the swirling snow. It was an 18-wheeler, a behemoth of a truck that looked like it could plow through a brick wall. The driver, a burly man with a bushy beard and a warm smile, pulled over and offered me a ride.

I climbed into the cab, grateful for the warmth and the company. The trucker, whose name was Joe, offered me a thermos of coffee and a sympathetic ear. I recounted my tale of woe, and he laughed heartily.

"Don't you worry, son," he said in a thick New York accent. "I'll get you to that radio station of yours, even if I have to drive this rig through a snowdrift the size of the Empire State Building."

True to his word, Joe navigated the treacherous roads with the skill of a seasoned pro. We dodged abandoned cars, plowed through snowdrifts, and even had a close encounter with a rogue snowplow. It was a wild ride, but we made it to the station just in time for my show.

I stumbled into the studio, still shivering and covered in snow. My co-host looked at me and burst out laughing.

"You look like a snowman who's been through a war," she said.

I didn't care. I was just grateful to be alive and alive. I launched into my show, my voice a little hoarse from the cold, but my spirits high. I shared my harrowing experience with the listeners, and they responded with an outpouring of support and sympathy.

The rest of the morning was a blur of news updates, weather reports, and calls from listeners who were also stranded in the blizzard. But through it all, I felt a sense of camaraderie with my audience, a shared experience that brought us closer together.

When the snow finally stopped falling, I was exhausted but exhilarated. I had survived a near-death experience, made it to work on time, and even managed to entertain my listeners in the process. And I had learned a valuable lesson: never underestimate the power of a blizzard, a good Samaritan, and a hot cup of coffee.

Chapter 13

Valentine's Day

Moving to Pittsburgh for a better talk radio show salary was a dream come true. But as Valentine's Day approached, the excitement of the new opportunity was overshadowed by the pang of guilt I felt for neglecting my girlfriend, Sarah.

Packing up the apartment had become a full-time job, leaving little time for romance. Mountains of boxes filled the living room, and the only sounds were the rustling of packing paper and the muffled thuds of furniture being moved. Sarah, usually bubbly and energetic, was subdued and withdrawn, her smile replaced by a frown.

"I feel like I'm just watching you move away," she said one evening, her voice barely above a whisper.

I tried to reassure her, telling her that this was a temporary setback, that we'd be settled in Pittsburgh in no time, and then we could finally start planning our future together. But my words rang hollow, even to my own ears.

On Valentine's Day, I awoke to the sound of silence. Sarah was gone, and a note lay on the kitchen table. It was a simple note, but the words cut deep: "I need someone who will be there for me, not just when it's convenient. I deserve more than just boxes and packing tape."

My heart sank. I had let my ambition blind me to the needs of the woman I loved. I had been so focused on my career that I had taken her for granted.

I knew I had to fix things. I raced to the airport, hoping to catch the last flight to Pittsburgh. Luckily, there was one seat left. As the plane took off, I felt a mix of excitement and dread. I was on my way to a new city, a new job, but I was leaving behind the woman I loved.

In Pittsburgh, I settled into my new apartment, unpacked the boxes, and started my new job. The show was a success, and I was making more money than I ever had before. But the thrill of success was short-lived. People surrounded me, but I felt alone.

One night, after a particularly long day, I decided to call Sarah. I poured my heart out to her, apologizing for my neglect and telling her how much I missed her.

She listened patiently, then said, "I know you're busy, Ed, but I need you to be here for me. I can't do this long distance thing anymore."

I knew she was right. I couldn't live without her. So, I made a decision. I quit my job in Pittsburgh and moved back to New York. I found a new job at a local radio station, and I finally made time for Sarah.

We got married a year later, and we're still together today. We learned a valuable lesson on Valentine's Day: love is more important than money or fame. And sometimes, the best way to show your love is to be there, not just when it's convenient, but always.

CHAPTER 14

TELEVISION REPORTER

The Pittsburgh Marathon was a big deal in the city, and I, as a local reporter for the television station, was excited to be part of the action. My assignment was to interview runners as they crossed the finish line, capturing their emotions and stories of triumph.

Armed with my microphone and a notepad, I positioned myself near the finish line, buzzing with anticipation. The first runner crossed the line, a young woman with a beaming smile and a triumphant fist pump. I approached her, eager to hear her story.

"Congratulations!" I exclaimed. "How was the race?"

The woman looked at me, confused. 'Wait, who are you?' she asked.

"I'm Ed, from Pittsburgh TV 6 News," I replied, holding up my microphone. "I'm here to interview you about your race."

The woman's smile widened. "Oh, wow! That's so cool! I've always wanted to be on TV."

Instead of interviewing her, she started interviewing me. She asked about my job, my experience reporting, and even my favorite pizza topping. I was taken aback, but I went along with it, amused by the unexpected turn of events.

As more runners crossed the finish line, the same thing happened. Instead of me interviewing them, they were interviewing me. They wanted to know about my life, my hobbies, and my thoughts on the marathon. I became the interviewee, not the interviewer.

Some of the questions were funny, some were insightful, and some were downright bizarre. One runner asked me if I believed in aliens, while another wanted to know my opinion on the meaning of life. I answered each question as honestly as I could, enjoying the impromptu conversations with these enthusiastic runners.

By the end of the day, I had interviewed dozens of runners, but they had interviewed me just as much. I learned about their training routines, their motivations for running, and their personal stories of overcoming challenges. I even learned a few new things about myself, thanks to their insightful questions.

As I left the finish line, I realized the Pittsburgh Marathon had been more than just a sporting event. It had been a human experience, a chance to connect with people from all walks of life and share stories of triumph and resilience. And while I hadn't interviewed the runners as planned, they had interviewed me. In the process, I had learned a valuable lesson: sometimes, the best stories are the ones that aren't planned.

Chapter 15

Hotline Rings

The red light above the studio door glowed ominously, signaling that I was live on air. It was the middle of my show, "The Ed Tyll Show," and I was in the midst of a heated debate with a caller about the merits of pineapple on pizza. Suddenly, the hotline phone flashed, indicating an important call. I excused myself to the caller and answered the hotline, bracing myself for breaking news or an irate listener.

"Ed Tyll here," I said, trying to sound composed despite the adrenaline coursing through my veins.

"Ed, my boy, how are you?" a voice boomed through the receiver. It was a voice I recognized instantly, the unmistakable baritone of Max Remington, the owner of a rival radio station across town.

"Max, what a surprise," I replied, my mind racing. Why was he calling me during my show? Was this some kind of prank?

"Listen, Ed," Max continued, his tone turning serious, "I've been listening to your show, and I'm impressed. You've got a real talent for connecting with your audience, and your humor is spot-on. I'm not gonna lie, you're giving my station a run for its money."

I couldn't help but grin. Flattery from a competitor was always welcome, even if it was a bit unexpected.

"Thanks, Max," I said. "I appreciate the compliment."

"But here's the thing, Ed," Max said, his voice dropping to a conspiratorial whisper. "I don't want to compete with you anymore. I want you on my team."

My heart skipped a beat. Was he offering me a job?

"What are you proposing, Max?" I asked, trying to keep my voice steady.

"I'm offering you a contract to host a lunchtime talk show on my station," Max said. "And I'm willing to double your current salary."

My jaw dropped. Double my salary? To host a show in Atlanta, the bustling media hub of the South? It was an offer I couldn't refuse.

But then, reality set in. I had a loyal audience in Pittsburgh, a comfortable routine, and a girlfriend who wasn't exactly thrilled about the idea of moving to a new city.

"Max, this is a lot to take in," I said, my voice filled with hesitation. "I need to think about it."

"Of course, Ed," Max replied, his tone understanding. "But don't take too long. This offer won't be on the table forever."

I hung up the phone, my mind buzzing with possibilities. The rest of my show was a blur. I fumbled through the remaining segments, my thoughts consumed by Max's offer.

After the show, I went home and told Sarah about the offer. She was initially hesitant, but after some discussion, we decided to take a leap of faith. We packed our bags, said goodbye to Pittsburgh, and headed south to Atlanta.

My new show was a hit. The Atlanta audience embraced my humor and wit, and the ratings soared. I was living the dream, hosting a successful talk radio show in a vibrant city, with the woman I loved by my side.

And every time I think of that fateful call from Max Remington, I can't help but smile. It was a moment that changed my life forever, a reminder that sometimes, the best opportunities come when you least expect them.

or to change the policy...
s its own talk station as big-sig-
LUX (540 AM) leaves standards
alk with new calls, WLIE. **John**
ott, formerly APD and executive
t WOR, New York is the PD. The
up is live and local during the
eatures **David Weiss** as host of
d's Morning News from 6:00 am
and **John Gomez** from 10:00 am
on. Rising star **Ed Tyll** returns to
York-area roots
ues his superb
rom hot talker
ring intense
ted talk radio
noon to 3:00
ve is anchored
teran talk host
l from 3:00 pm

Ed Tyll

This **Stan Henry**-owned and
ation is going to be one to
FO, San Francisco morning
dgers is helping the widow of
gent **Mike Spann**. Rodgers
non Spann was having finan-

Rising Star

CHAPTER 16

YANKEE BOY

Stepping off the plane in Atlanta, the heat and humidity hit me like a wall. It was a far cry from the chilly winters of New York, but I was ready for a change. I was here to take on the lunchtime talk radio slot at one of the city's top stations, and I was determined to make a splash.

My first day at the station was a whirlwind of introductions, paperwork, and technical jargon. The staff was friendly, but I could sense a hint of skepticism beneath their Southern hospitality. After all, I was a Yankee, an outsider, coming in to shake up their established order.

As I walked into the studio for my first show, the program director, a jovial man with a thick drawl, clapped me on the back. "Welcome to Atlanta, son. We're excited to have you here. But fair warning, we like our radio hosts with a little Southern charm."

I grinned. "Don't worry, I'll bring the charm. And the energy. And maybe a few Yankees jokes, just to keep things interesting."

The program director chuckled. "We'll see about that, Yankee. We'll see about that."

The moment the "On Air" light flashed, I was off to the races. I introduced myself to the listeners, cracked a few jokes about the weather (it was hot, y'all), and launched into my first topic: the best places to get barbecue in Atlanta.

The phones lit up instantly. Callers were eager to share their favorite barbecue joints, their secret recipes, and their opinions on the proper way to cook ribs. I was in my element, engaging with the audience, cracking jokes, and keeping the conversation flowing.

But as the show progressed, I noticed a recurring theme in the callers' comments. They kept referring to me as "the Yankee," with a mix of amusement and bemusement. Some callers even playfully teased me about my fast-paced speech and my tendency to use words like "wicked" and "awesome."

At first I was a bit surprised. Was I being mocked? Was my Northern accent and energetic style too much for the laid-back Southern audience?

But then I realized the teasing was good-natured. The listeners were simply acknowledging my outsider status, and they were doing it with humor and warmth. In fact, the more they teased me, the more they seemed to embrace me.

By the end of the show, I had been officially dubbed "the Yankee with the gift of gab." It was a nickname that stuck, and I wore it proudly. I had found my place in the Atlanta radio landscape, and I was loving every minute of it.

Over the next few weeks, my show became a lunchtime staple for Atlanta listeners. I tackled a wide range of topics, from local news and politics to pop culture and relationship advice. I even started a weekly segment called "Yankee vs. Rebel," where I debated Southern traditions and customs with a local co-host.

The show was a hit, and I quickly became a beloved figure in the Atlanta community. I learned to appreciate the slower pace of life, the delicious Southern cuisine, and the warm hospitality of the people. And while I never lost my Yankee accent or my energetic style, I learned to adapt to my new surroundings, adding a touch of Southern charm to my on-air persona.

In the end, moving to Atlanta was the best decision I ever made.

I found a new home, a new audience, and a new appreciation for the Southern way of life. And while I may always be known as "the Yankee," I'm proud to be a part of the Atlanta radio family.

52

CHAPTER 17

THE SHOCKING

The aroma of freshly brewed coffee filled my kitchen as I unfolded the morning newspaper, a ritual I cherished almost as much as my first sip of caffeine. But this morning was different. Staring back at me from the front page was a photo of yours truly, accompanied by a headline that made me do a double-take: "The Shocking Ed Tyll: Is He the Future of Talk Radio?"

My heart pounded in my chest as I read the article, a mix of exhilaration and disbelief washing over me. The journalist had captured my essence perfectly, describing my "outrageously hilarious" hosting style, my "quick wit and sharp tongue," and my "uncanny ability to connect with listeners on a personal level."

They even delved into my biography, recounting my humble beginnings in community radio, my rise to fame on the local airwaves, and my recent move to a major talk radio station in Atlanta. The article painted a picture of a young, ambitious broadcaster who was unafraid to push boundaries and challenge the status quo.

But it was the final paragraph that truly sent shivers down my spine. The journalist suggested that I represented the "future of talk radio in America," a bold claim that both flattered and terrified me.

As I finished reading the article, a wave of emotions washed over me. I was proud of what I had accomplished, grateful for the recognition, and excited about the possibilities that lay ahead. But I was also acutely aware of the pressure that came with such high praise. Can I meet expectations? Would I be able to maintain my unique style and continue to captivate audiences?

The rest of the day was a blur of phone calls, emails, and congratulatory messages. My colleagues at the station were buzzing with excitement, and my boss even gave me a raise. But amidst the celebration, I couldn't shake the feeling that I was standing at a crossroads.

I knew that this article had the potential to change my career trajectory, to open doors I had never even dreamed of. But it also meant that I would be under intense scrutiny, my every word and action analyzed and dissected by critics and fans alike.

As I sat in the studio that afternoon, preparing for my show, I took a deep breath and reminded myself of why I had gotten into talk radio in the first place. It was about connecting with people, sharing stories, and making them laugh. It was about being myself, even if that meant being a bit shocking at times.

I put on my headphones, adjusted my microphone, and smiled. The "On Air" light flashed, and I was off to the races. I launched into my show with renewed energy, my voice filled with the same passion and humor that had earned me the moniker "The Shocking Ed Tyll."

The calls poured in, the listeners were engaged, and the laughter was infectious. I knew then that I had nothing to fear. I was ready to embrace the future of talk radio, to continue pushing boundaries, and to keep making people laugh, one shockingly hilarious show at a time.

The Shocking

Chapter 18

Obstinate Author

It was a particularly frustrating day on "The Ed Tyll Show." My guest for the afternoon was a renowned author, known for his controversial opinions and enigmatic personality. I had high hopes for a lively and thought-provoking discussion, but from the moment he came on air, it was clear that he had other plans.

No matter what question I threw at him, he would dodge, deflect, and digress. He spoke in vague generalities, offered cryptic non-answers, and even resorted to quoting obscure philosophers. It was like trying to nail jelly to a wall.

My frustration grew with each passing minute. The listeners were getting restless, the phones were silent, and the tension in the studio was palpable. I tried everything I could think of to engage him, from humor to flattery to outright provocation. But nothing worked.

Finally, after what felt like an eternity of circular conversations and pointless tangents, I snapped.

"Listen," I said, my voice rising with exasperation, "I'm trying to have a meaningful conversation here, but you're not giving me anything to work with. It's like I'm talking to a brick wall. No, scratch that. It's like I'm talking to Popeye the Sailor Man."

There was a moment of stunned silence on the other end of the line. Then, the author's voice, cold and clipped, came through the speakers.

"I beg your pardon?" he said, clearly offended.

"You heard me," I retorted. "You're about as communicative as a cartoon character. At least Popeye would give me a straight answer, even if it was just 'I yam what I yam.'"

The author scoffed. "I see. Well, Mr. Tyll, if that's how you feel, then perhaps we should end this interview."

And with that, he hung up.

The dial tone blared through the speakers, a deafening silence filling the studio. I sat there, stunned and speechless. I had never had a guest hang up on me on air before.

The phones lit up instantly. Callers were flooding the lines, some expressing outrage at my behavior, others defending my right to call out a difficult guest. The social media was abuzz with comments and opinions, and the hashtag #Popeyegate was trending nationwide.

The incident became a talking point for days, with other radio hosts weighing in on the ethics of on-air confrontations. Some praised me for standing up to a difficult guest, while others criticized me for being unprofessional and disrespectful.

In the end, the controversy only served to boost my show's ratings. Listeners tuned in to see what I would say next, eager for more drama and entertainment. And while I regretted losing my temper, I couldn't help but feel a sense of satisfaction at having stood my ground.

The lesson I learned that day was a valuable one: never underestimate the power of a cartoon character reference. And always be prepared for a guest to walk out on you, especially if you compare them to Popeye the Sailor Man.

CHAPTER 19

THE WEATHER GUY

The opportunity for a good prank presented itself during my afternoon talk radio show. My guest was the local TV weatherman, a man known for his seriousness and professionalism. I decided to have some fun with him, asking him a series of increasingly absurd questions about the weather.

"So, Mark," I began, "what can you tell us about the upcoming storm?"

Mark, ever the professional, launched into a detailed explanation of the storm's expected path, wind speeds, and potential impact. I listened patiently, waiting for my moment to strike.

"Interesting," I said, feigning seriousness. "But what about the effect of the storm on, say, the migratory patterns of squirrels?"

Mark blinked, momentarily confused. "Well, I'm not sure about squirrels specifically, but the storm is expected to cause significant disruptions to wildlife in general."

"And what about the impact on the price of, say, bananas?" I continued, pushing my luck.

Mark chuckled nervously. "I don't think the storm will have a direct impact on banana prices, but it could potentially disrupt supply chains, leading to price fluctuations."

"And what about the chances of the storm causing, say, a zombie apocalypse?" I asked, fully committed to the bit.

Mark let out a genuine laugh. "Now you're just being silly, Ed. There's no scientific evidence to suggest that the storm will cause a zombie apocalypse."

"But you can't say it's impossible, can you?" I pressed, enjoying his discomfort.

Mark sighed. "Look, I'm here to talk about the weather, not hypothetical scenarios involving squirrels, bananas, and zombies."

"But the weather is full of surprises, Mark," I said, my voice dripping with mock seriousness. "Who knows what strange and unexpected events it might bring?"

The rest of the interview was a hilarious mix of serious weather analysis and my increasingly ridiculous questions. Mark handled it like a champ, maintaining his composure while clearly being aware that he was being teased.

Later that evening, I was watching the local news when Mark appeared for his weather segment. He started with the usual forecast, then paused and looked directly into the camera.

"And to Ed Tyll, who earlier today asked me a series of very silly questions about the weather," Mark said with a smile, "I just want to say, rest assured, there will be no zombie apocalypse caused by this storm. But I can't say the same for the price of bananas."

The audience laughed and I couldn't help but grin. My prank had been a success, and it had brought a little bit of lightheartedness to the serious topic of weather.

The next day, my phone was buzzing with calls and messages from listeners who had enjoyed the prank. Even Mark called me, laughing and thanking me for making him laugh.

That day, I learned that a little bit of humor can go a long way, even in the most unexpected places. And I also learned that you can never underestimate the power of a good prank, especially when it's targeted at a serious weatherman.

CHAPTER 20

BLEACHER SEATS

Ascending to the coveted position of Program Director was a dream realized, a testament to years of hard work, dedication, and countless hours spent honing my craft. But with great power comes great responsibility, and a vision. My vision? To revolutionize the way talk radio was experienced, to create an immersive and interactive environment where the audience wasn't just listening, but actively participating in the show. And so the bleacher studio idea was born.

The concept was simple yet audacious: build a state-of-the-art studio with bleacher seating for a live audience. Listeners could come watch the show in person, interact with me and the guests, and even have the opportunity to voice their opinions on air. It was a bold move, a departure from the traditional, isolated radio booths, but I was convinced it would be a game-changer.

Construction began, and the excitement was palpable. The studio was designed to resemble a miniature sports arena, complete with a central stage for me and the guests, rows of comfortable bleachers for the audience, and a giant screen displaying call-in numbers and social media feeds.

The grand opening was a night to remember. The studio was packed with eager listeners, the atmosphere electric with anticipation. As I entered the stage, the crowd erupted in cheers. It was a rock concert meets town hall meeting, and I was the conductor of this symphony of voices.

The show was a whirlwind of energy and spontaneity. I fielded questions from the audience, interviewed guests on the stage, and even had a few brave souls come up to the microphone to share their thoughts on air. The bleachers were alive with laughter, applause, and the occasional heckle.

One particularly memorable moment involved a heated debate between two audience members about Bigfoot's existence. The argument grew so passionate that I had to step in and mediate, eventually suggesting that we take a vote from the entire audience. The result was a resounding "yes" in favor of Bigfoot, much to the delight of the believer and the chagrin of the skeptic.

The bleacher studio quickly became a success, drawing crowds from all over the city. Listeners loved the opportunity to be part of the show, interact with me and the guests, and feel like they were part of a community. The ratings soared, and the station became a local phenomenon.

Of course, there were challenges. Managing a live audience during a broadcast required a delicate balance of control and spontaneity. There were technical glitches, unruly guests, and the occasional heckler who had to be escorted out by security. But overall, the bleacher studio was a resounding success.

It revolutionized the way talk radio was experienced, creating a dynamic and engaging environment that brought listeners closer to the action. And for me, it was a dream come true, a chance to connect with my audience on a deeper level and to share the laughter, the debates, and the occasional absurdity of life with a live audience.

Chapter 21

Mardi Gras

Landing a new talk radio job in New Orleans was a dream come true, especially with the timing coinciding perfectly with the city's most iconic celebration: Mardi Gras. The energy, the music, the vibrant colors – it was a sensory overload in the best possible way. And as the host of the afternoon drive-time show, I had a front-row seat to the madness.

The radio station was located right on Bourbon Street, the heart of the French Quarter and the epicenter of Mardi Gras revelry. Our studio had a large window overlooking the street, allowing passersby to see us in action. And boy, did they see us in action.

From the moment my show started, the crowds outside went wild. They pressed their faces against the glass, waving, cheering, and shouting my name. Beads, doubloons, and even the occasional coconut flew through the air, landing in a colorful pile on the studio floor.

But the real showstopper was the lingerie. Bras of all shapes, sizes, and colors were flung towards the window, their owners hoping to catch my attention. It was a sight to behold, a testament to the uninhibited spirit of Mardi Gras.

I tried to maintain my composure, but it was difficult with a constant barrage of beads and bras whizzing past my head. My co-host, a seasoned New Orleans native, was unfazed, laughing and catching the flying objects with ease.

"Welcome to Mardi Gras, Ed," she said with a grin. "This is just the beginning."

And she was right. As the day went on, the crowds became larger and more boisterous. The music from the street bands grew louder, and the aroma of fried food and spilled beer filled the air.

I embraced the chaos, incorporating it into my show. I interviewed callers who were celebrating in the streets, played Mardi Gras-themed trivia games, and even attempted to catch a few beads myself (with varying degrees of success).

At one point, a group of revelers outside started chanting my name, demanding that I join them in the festivities. I hesitated, but my co-host gave me a nudge.

"Go on, Ed," she said. "It's Mardi Gras. Live a little."

So, I did. I stepped out of the studio and into the throng of people, a microphone in one hand and a string of beads in the other. The crowd went wild, cheering and showering me with beads and kisses.

For the next hour, I was part of the parade. I danced with strangers, sang along with the bands, and even caught a few bras myself (which I promptly returned to their owners). It was a surreal and unforgettable experience, a true baptism by beads.

When I finally returned to the studio, I was exhausted but exhilarated. I had never felt so alive, so connected to a city and its people. And I knew I had found my home in New Orleans.

The rest of my time at the station was filled with equally wild and hilarious moments. I interviewed musicians, chefs, and even a voodoo priestess. I covered local news stories, debated controversial topics, and always kept the audience entertained.

But it was the first Mardi Gras I will never forget. It was the day I truly became a part of New Orleans, the day I learned to embrace the city's unique spirit and let the good times roll.

Tuesday, March 27,
VARIETY
MONDAY, NOVEMBER 10, 199

SHOCK JOCK
TYLL AT KABC

The on-again, off-again deal
between KABC radio and its long-
speculated new personali-
Jock Ed Tyll

ENTERTAINMENT SUNDAY, OCTOBER 24, 1993

40 DETROIT FREE PRESS

LA radio personality moves
his saucy talk show to Detroit

By JOHN SMYNTEK
FREE PRESS STAFF WRITER

At best, he's the second coming
of Arthur Godfrey.
At worst, he's merely the latest
voice attempting to make "FM
young talk" work in the Detroit
radio market.
That great either/or, begins
Monday a little before 11 a.m.
when Ed Tyll launches his nation-
ally syndicated midday show on
WKRK-FM (97.1). The national
portion airs noon-3 p.m.; the post-
Howard Stern to noon segment
will only be heard locally.
Tyll comes from Los Angeles,
where he hosted a syndicated late-
night talk fest. It was often the
most talked-about national night
owl offering among radio cogno-

Ed Tyll comes off as
energetic, thoughtful,
spirited, engaging and
knowing exactly what he
wants to do in his radio
career. ... And for a guy
who occasionally will
discuss circumcision,
beach nudity and othe
saucy topics on the a
it may surprise some
that his broadcast h
is '40s-'50s icon ar
publicly straight-la
Arthur Godfrey.

Saucy Show

CHAPTER 22

LUNCHTIME LOVE

The phones were buzzing on my talk radio show, "The Ed Tyll Show," as listeners eagerly called in to share their most embarrassing moments. It was a segment we called "Tales of Humiliation," and it never failed to deliver cringe-worthy yet hilarious stories. But one particular call that day took the cake, a tale so outrageous and absurd that it became an instant classic.

The caller, a man named Dave, recounted a recent escapade that had turned into a public spectacle. Dave, a married man with a wandering eye, had been carrying on a clandestine affair with a coworker. Their trysts usually took place during their lunch breaks, in the secluded parking lot of a nearby park.

One fateful afternoon, Dave and his paramour were enjoying a particularly passionate rendezvous in his car. Things were heating up, and they were so engrossed in their activities that they failed to notice a slight incline in the parking spot.

As their passion peaked, Dave's car, unbeknownst to them, began to roll slowly towards a nearby tree. The couple, oblivious to the impending disaster, continued their amorous activities, their moans and giggles masking the sound of the car's movement.

Suddenly, with a bone-jarring thud, the car came to an abrupt stop. The impact jolted Dave and his companion out of their passionate haze. They looked around in confusion, trying to figure out what had happened.

That's when they realized, to their horror, that the car had rolled into a tree, trapping them both inside. The doors were jammed shut, the windows were partially open, and they were stuck in a compromising position, their clothes in disarray.

Worse, a group of joggers had witnessed the entire incident. They were standing nearby, their mouths agape, their eyes wide with shock and amusement.

Dave and his co-worker were mortified. They tried to cover themselves with whatever they could find, but it was too late. The joggers had already pulled out their phones and were snapping photos and videos of the scene.

Within minutes, the police and fire department arrived. Fire-fighters used the Jaws of Life to open the car doors. Dave and his companion were extracted from the vehicle, their faces red with embarrassment.

The story quickly made its way to the local news, complete with blurry photos and eyewitness accounts. Dave and his co-worker became the talk of the town, their names forever associated with the infamous "Lunchtime Love Trap."

As Dave finished his story, the studio was filled with uproarious laughter. The listeners were calling in, sharing their own stories of embarrassing moments and offering words of sympathy (and a few jokes) to Dave.

I couldn't help but feel a pang of sympathy for Dave. While his actions were certainly questionable, the public humiliation he had endured was punishment enough. But the story was just too funny to ignore, a perfect example of life's unexpected twists and turns.

The "Lunchtime Love Trap" became a legendary tale on "The Ed Tyll Show," a cautionary reminder to always check your parking brake and to be aware of your surroundings, even in the heat of the moment. And it also served as a testament to the power of humor, the ability to find laughter even in the most embarrassing and absurd situations.

CHAPTER 23

CHICAGO, CHICAGO

The vibrant energy of New Orleans, with its lively music scene and the intoxicating allure of Mardi Gras, had been my home for years. As a talk radio host, I had carved out a niche for myself, entertaining listeners with my quick wit, controversial opinions, and the occasional on-air prank. But when a call came from a legendary Chicago talk radio station, offering me a chance to join their lineup, I knew I was at a crossroads.

The offer was tempting, to say the least. A significant pay raise, a larger audience, and the opportunity to work alongside some of the biggest names in the industry. But leaving New Orleans, the city that had embraced me and my brand of radio, was a tough pill to swallow.

The Chicago station, however, was not taking no for an answer. They flew me up for a weekend of wining and dining, determined to woo me away from the Big Easy. My first night in the Windy City, I was whisked away to a swanky steakhouse, where I was treated to a feast fit for a king. The general manager, a charismatic man with a booming voice, regaled me with tales of the station's storied history, its legendary hosts, and its commitment to pushing the boundaries of talk radio.

The next day, I was given a tour of the station, a state-of-the-art facility that was a far cry from the cramped and outdated studio I was used to in New Orleans. The control room was a technological marvel, the on-air studios were spacious and comfortable, and the staff was buzzing with energy and enthusiasm.

That evening, I was taken to a Cubs game at Wrigley Field, where I experienced the electric atmosphere of a packed stadium and the thrill of a walk-off home run. The general manager, sitting beside me, leaned in and said, "Imagine hosting your show in a city that's passionate about sports, about ideas, about life. Imagine the possibilities."

By the end of the weekend, I was hooked. The combination of the station's prestige, the city's vibrant energy, and the promise of a new challenge was too much to resist. I accepted their offer, and within weeks, I was packing my bags and saying goodbye to New Orleans.

The move to Chicago was a whirlwind. I had to adjust to a new city, a new audience, and a new style of radio. The Chicago listeners were more opinionated, more politically engaged, and more demanding than their New Orleans counterparts. But I rose to the challenge, adapting my style to fit the city's unique vibe.

My show quickly became a hit, thanks to my quick wit, my willingness to tackle controversial topics, and my ability to connect with listeners on a personal level. I interviewed politicians, celebrities, and everyday people with fascinating stories to tell. I debated hot-button issues, sparked lively discussions, and always kept the audience entertained.

And while I missed the warmth and charm of New Orleans, I found a new home in Chicago. The city embraced me, and I embraced it. I became a regular at Cubs games, a connoisseur of deep-dish pizza, and a die-hard fan of the city's vibrant music scene.

Looking back on that fateful weekend in Chicago, I realize it was a turning point in my career. It was the moment I stepped out of my comfort zone and into the big leagues of talk radio. And while I'll always cherish my time in New Orleans, I'm grateful for the opportunity to have been wined and dined away to a city that challenged me, inspired me, and ultimately helped me become the broadcaster I am today.

Good Listener

Chapter 24

Backstage

The chill of a Chicago Thanksgiving night was the perfect backdrop for a rock 'n' roll extravaganza. I had scored tickets to see my favorite band, the legendary "Rock Gods," and I was taking my new girlfriend, Emily, on a date she'd never forget.

Emily, a vibrant and adventurous woman with a passion for music, was practically bouncing with excitement as we made our way to the packed arena. The energy in the air was electric, the crowd buzzing with anticipation. As the lights dimmed and the first chords echoed through the stadium, we were swept away by the raw power of the music.

The band was on fire, their performance a mesmerizing blend of virtuosity and showmanship. The lead singer, a charismatic figure with a voice that could melt steel, commanded the stage with a presence that was both electrifying and captivating. Emily and I were lost in the moment, singing along, dancing, and sharing stolen glances.

After the encore, a member of the band's crew, who recognized me from my radio show, approached us. He offered us backstage passes, an invitation we eagerly accepted.

Backstage was a whirlwind of activity, with roadies dismantling equipment, band members chatting with friends and family, and the lingering scent of sweat and adrenaline. We were led to a private lounge where the band was relaxing after their performance.

The lead singer, still radiating rock star charisma, greeted us warmly. He complimented me on my show, expressed his admiration for Emily's infectious energy, and then, to our astonishment, invited us to join him and the band for Thanksgiving dinner.

"There's a famous restaurant nearby that's opening up just for us," he said with a grin. "It's a tradition we have after every Thanksgiving show. You guys in?"

We were speechless. Dinner with the Rock Gods? On Thanksgiving night? It was a dream come true.

We arrived at the restaurant, a dimly lit, upscale establishment with a reputation for serving the city's elite. The band, dressed in casual clothes and looking surprisingly down-to-earth, welcomed us like old friends.

The dinner was a blur of laughter, stories, and delicious food. We talked about music, life, and everything in between. The band members shared hilarious anecdotes from their touring days, and we exchanged stories about our own experiences in the entertainment industry.

I was starstruck, but Emily was in her element. She charmed the band with her wit and intelligence, and they seemed genuinely delighted by her company. I watched with pride as she effortlessly held her own in this surreal and unexpected situation.

As the night drew to a close, the lead singer raised a glass in our honor. "To Ed and Emily," he said, "two of the coolest people we've met in a long time. Thanks for joining us tonight."

We thanked him and the band for their hospitality, still reeling from the experience. As we walked out of the restaurant and into the chilly night air, Emily turned to me with a smile that lit up the entire city.

"Best Thanksgiving ever," she said, her eyes sparkling.

I couldn't agree more. It was a night we would never forget, a magical blend of music, romance, and unexpected encounters with rock 'n' roll royalty. And as we walked hand-in-hand down the Chicago streets, I knew that this was just the beginning of our adventure together.

On Location

CHAPTER 25

COMP SEATS

Being a talk radio host in Chicago came with its perks, and one of the most delightful was the occasional freebie. One day, a pair of tickets landed on my desk: front-row seats to Paul McCartney at Soldier Field. It was a dream come true for any music lover, and I knew just the person to share this experience with – my new girl-friend, Emily.

Emily, with her infectious laughter and shared passion for music, was the perfect companion for such a special occasion. I called her up, my voice brimming with excitement, and asked her to join me for the concert. She squealed with delight, and we eagerly marked the date on our calendars.

But as luck would have it, another pair of tickets arrived the following week: VIP passes to Janet Jackson at the New World Theater. And the kicker? Both concerts were the same night.

Now, most people would have been content with attending one of these legendary shows. But I, ever the ambitious optimist, saw an opportunity for a truly epic musical adventure.

I called Emily again, this time with a slightly nervous chuckle. "How would you feel about a double-header?" I asked.

She paused, then laughed. "A double-header? You mean, like, two concerts in one night?"

"Exactly," I replied. "Paul McCartney and Janet Jackson, back to back. It'll be a night we'll never forget."

Emily, always up for an adventure, agreed. We hatched a plan: see Paul McCartney first, then race across town to catch Janet Jackson. It was a logistical challenge, but we were determined to make it work.

The night of the concerts arrived, and we were off to Soldier Field, dressed to the nines and buzzing with anticipation. Paul McCartney's performance was everything we had hoped for and more. He played all the classics, captivating the crowd with his timeless melodies and stage presence. We sang, danced and marveled at the fact that we were witnessing a living legend in action.

As the final notes of "Hey Jude" faded away, we reluctantly tore ourselves away from the concert and raced towards the exit. We hailed a cab, the driver looking at us incredulously as we explained our plan.

"Two concerts in one night?" he asked, shaking his head. "You kids are crazy."

We laughed and urged him to drive faster. We arrived at the New World Theater just as Janet Jackson was taking the stage. We rushed to our seats, breathless but exhilarated.

Janet's performance was a high-energy spectacle, filled with elaborate choreography, dazzling costumes, and infectious beats. We danced, sang, and revealed the sheer joy of the music. Black Cat, always my fave.

As the night came to an end, we stumbled out of the theater, exhausted but elated. We had pulled off the impossible, attending two iconic concerts in one night. It was a testament to our shared love of music, our adventurous spirit, and our willingness to embrace the unexpected.

And as we walked hand-in-hand through the quiet Chicago streets, the city lights twinkling above us, I knew that this was a night we would cherish forever. It was a reminder that life is full of surprises, and that sometimes, the most memorable experiences are the ones that happen spontaneously.

Making Commercials

CHAPTER 26

COOLEST HOTEL

The biting wind howled through the streets of Chicago, whipping snow into a frenzy as I stepped out of the taxi. It was a blizzard of epic proportions, the kind that makes you question your life choices as you struggle to maintain your footing on the icy sidewalk. But I was undeterred, my excitement outweighing the discomfort. I was finally in Chicago, the city of big shoulders, deep-dish pizza, and legendary talk radio.

My destination was the Chicago House, a historic landmark on the Magnificent Mile. As I entered the grand lobby, adorned with crystal chandeliers and plush velvet furniture, I felt a sense of awe. This was a place where legends had walked, where history had been made.

Checking in, I couldn't help but mention my lifelong fandom of The Rolling Stones. The receptionist, a friendly woman with a knowing smile, informed me that I had been upgraded to a very special suite.

"You're in luck," she said. "We've put you in the Rolling Stones Suite."

My heart skipped a beat. "The Rolling Stones Suite?" I repeated, barely able to contain my excitement.

"Yes," she confirmed. "It's the actual suite where the band stayed during their first visit to Chicago in 1964."

I was speechless. As a die-hard Stones fan, this was beyond my wildest dreams. I thanked the receptionist profusely and practically ran to the elevator.

The suite was everything I had imagined and more. It was spacious and elegant, with a vintage charm that transported me back in time. The walls were adorned with framed photos of the band, their youthful faces beaming with the energy and rebellious spirit that would define a generation.

I explored the suite, imagining Mick Jagger strutting across the living room, Keith Richards strumming his guitar on the balcony, and the rest of the band indulging in the rock 'n' roll lifestyle. I could almost hear the faint echoes of their music, laughter, and camaraderie.

That night, I slept in the same bed where Mick Jagger had once slept, dreaming of wild nights, sold-out stadiums, and the timeless allure of rock 'n' roll.

The next morning, I woke up feeling like a rockstar myself. I walked down the Magnificent Mile, the snow still falling but my spirits were high. I had a new job, a new city, and a newfound connection to my musical idols.

As I started my new life in Chicago, I often thought back to that snowy night at the Chicago House. It was a reminder that dreams can come true, even in the most unexpected ways. And it was a testament to the power of music, the ability to connect people across generations and inspire them to live life to the fullest.

CHAPTER 27

FORMAT CHANGE

The news was like a gut punch. My beloved talk radio station, my Chicago home of "The Ed Tyll Show," was going all sports, leaving me and my listeners in the dust. It was a devastating blow, a sign of the changing times and the dwindling popularity of traditional talk radio.

But amidst the despair, a glimmer of hope emerged. A local rock station in the suburbs, "Rockin' 95.5," was looking to expand their programming and saw me as the perfect fit to launch their very first talk radio show. It was an unexpected offer, a chance to reinvent myself and reach a new audience.

I accepted the challenge, eager to prove that my voice still had a place in the radio landscape. I poured my heart and soul into crafting the show, choosing the name "Ed's Rockin' Rant" to reflect its unique blend of hard rock music and provocative conversation.

The first episode was a nerve-wracking experience. I was used to the familiar comfort of my old studio, the loyal listeners who knew my every quirk and habit. But this was a new world, a new audience, and I had to find my footing.

But as the show progressed, I found myself falling into a groove. I talked about music, politics, life, and everything in between, my voice infused with the same passion and humor that had captivated my listeners for years.

The response was overwhelming. Rock fans embraced my show, appreciating my knowledge of music and my willingness to tackle controversial topics with a rock 'n' roll attitude. The station's ratings soared, and "Ed's Rockin' Rant" quickly became a local favorite.

One day, I received a call from a writer at "Suburban Rock," a popular local magazine. They were interested in doing a profile on me, the "rock 'n' roll talk radio pioneer" who had dared to challenge the status quo.

The interview was a blast. We talked about my career, my love of music, and my vision for the future of talk radio. The writer was clearly impressed, and the article that appeared in the magazine was glowing.

"Ed Tyll," the article declared, "is a breath of fresh air in a world of stale talk radio. He's a rock star with a microphone, and he's here to stay."

Reading those words, I couldn't help but grin. The transition from talk radio to rock radio had been a gamble, but it had paid off in ways I could never have imagined. I had found a new home, a new audience, and a new platform to share my voice and my passion.

And as I looked out at the city from my studio window, the lights twinkling in the distance, I knew that this was just the beginning. The rock 'n' roll revolution had begun, and I was it's fearless leader.

Chapter 28

Sunshine Calls

The Florida sun was beating down on the palm-lined streets of Orlando as I stepped out of the airport, a sense of excitement and anticipation bubbling within me. I had just been offered a once-in-a-lifetime opportunity: to join the launch of a brand-new talk radio station and host my own midday show.

The station was making waves in the industry, boasting state-of-the-art facilities, a roster of top-tier talent, and a bold vision for the future of talk radio. They were aiming to create a station that was informative, entertaining, and unapologetically Floridian.

My show, aptly titled "The Ed Tyll Show," was slated to follow the biggest morning show in the market, a powerhouse host with sharp wit and engaging banter. The pressure was on to deliver a show that was just as captivating, but with my own unique brand of humor and irreverence.

I spent weeks meticulously planning the format, brainstorming topics, and lining up guests. I wanted to create a show that was a reflection of my personality, a wild and unpredictable ride that would keep listeners on the edge of their seats.

Launch day arrived and I was a bundle of nerves. I had never hosted a show in such a high-pressure environment, and the thought of following the morning juggernaut was daunting. But as I walked into the studio, greeted by the smiling faces of my producers and the state-of-the-art equipment, a wave of confidence washed over me.

The moment the "On Air" light flashed, I was off to the races. I launched into my opening monologue, a mix of current events, pop culture commentary, and self-deprecating humor. The phones lit up instantly, and the listeners were hooked.

My show was a whirlwind of energy and spontaneity. I interviewed eccentric guests, debated controversial topics, and engaged in hilarious on-air antics. One day, I challenged a listener to a live karaoke battle, our voices echoing through the studio as we belted out classic rock anthems. Another time, I hosted a "Florida Man" segment, where listeners called in to share their most outrageous encounters with the state's infamous residents.

The audience loved it. They embraced my humor, my irreverence, and my willingness to push the boundaries of traditional talk radio. The ratings soared, and "The Ed Tyll Show" quickly became a midday staple for Florida listeners.

As the show's popularity grew, so did my profile in the community. I was invited to host charity events, appear on local television programs, and even judge a bikini contest (a perk I certainly didn't complain about).

But the real reward was the connection I felt with my listeners. They became like family, sharing their stories, opinions and laughter with me daily. I had found my tribe, and they had found theirs in me.

The success of "The Ed Tyll Show" was a testament to the power of personality-driven radio. In a world of pre-packaged content and cookie-cutter formats, my show stood out as a unique and authentic voice. It was a reminder that radio, at its best, is a conversation, a connection between a host and their listeners.

And as I looked out at the skyline from my studio window, the sun setting over the ocean, I couldn't help but feel a sense of gratitude. I had been given a chance to do what I loved, to make people laugh, and to be a part of something truly special. The Florida sun had indeed shone brightly on my career, and I was basking in its warm glow.

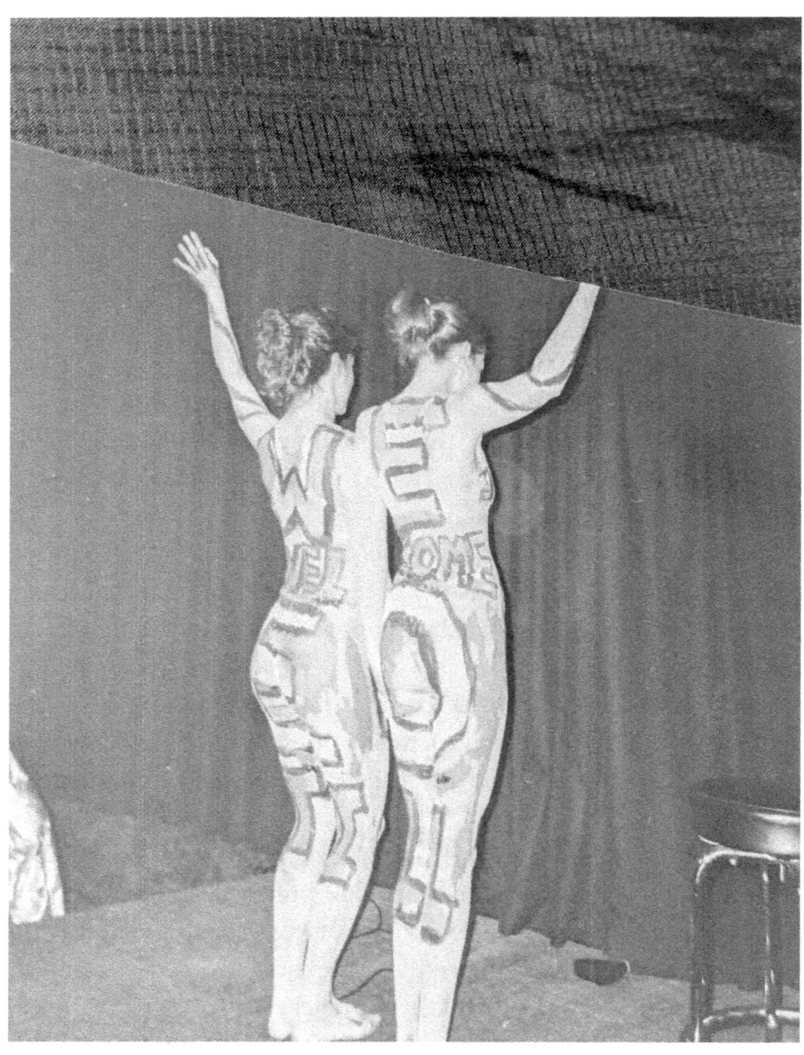

Body Painted Welcome

CHAPTER 29

OPENING NIGHT

The excitement crackled in the air like electricity as I prepared for my first live talk radio promotion, a night of music, mayhem, and free drinks at the hottest nightclub in Orlando. My show, "The Ed Tyll Show," had been a hit on the airwaves, captivating listeners with my irreverent humor, insightful commentary, and knack for getting into trouble. But tonight, I was taking things to the next level.

As I arrived at the club, the energy was palpable. The line snaked around the block, filled with eager listeners ready to party with their favorite radio host. The club itself was a sensory overload, with flashing lights, thumping bass, and a crowd buzzing with anticipation.

My entourage, a motley crew of friends and fellow radio personalities, was ready to rock. We were armed with microphones, a portable sound system, and a seemingly endless supply of energy. As I took the stage, the crowd erupted in cheers, their voices echoing through the club.

My show was a whirlwind of live interviews, impromptu games, and audience participation. I talked about everything from current events to pop culture to the best places to get a hangover cure in Orlando. The audience loved it, hanging on every word and responding with laughter and cheers.

The highlight of the night was a live performance by a local band, their music electrifying the crowd and turning the club into a mosh pit of sweaty bodies and joyous abandon. I even joined them on stage for a few songs, my lack of musical talent adding to the comedic chaos.

As the night wore on, the party moved from the club to the streets of Orlando. My entourage and I hopped from bar to bar, each stopping a new adventure. We danced with strangers, sang karaoke, and even got into a friendly (and slightly drunken) debate with a group of college students about the meaning of life.

By the time the sun rose over the city, we were exhausted but exhilarated. We had created a night of memories that would last a lifetime, a testament to the power of live radio and the infectious energy of a good party.

The next day, the local news was buzzing with the story of my wild night. The headlines screamed "Talk Radio Host Throws Epic Party," "Ed Tyll Takes Orlando by Storm," and "The Night the City Didn't Sleep." The promotion had been a resounding success, solidifying my reputation as the most entertaining and unpredictable radio host in Florida.

As I sat in my studio, reflecting on the previous night's events, I couldn't help but grin. I had taken a chance, stepped outside the comfort zone of the studio, and created a night of pure, unadulterated fun. And in doing so, I had connected with my listeners on a deeper level, proving that radio could be more than just a voice coming out of a box. It could be a catalyst for community, laughter, and unforgettable memories.

And as for the entourage, well, let's just say they were already asking when the next live promotion was happening. After all, it was an amazing launch.

Newsmaker

Chapter 30

Bungee Jumping Host

The sun beat down on International Drive, Orlando's bustling tourist hub, as I prepared for a radio broadcast unlike any other. My show, known for its spontaneous and often outrageous stunts, was going to be hosted live from the epicenter of an adrenaline junkie's paradise: a bungee jump platform.

My producers had met the idea with a mix of excitement and trepidation. On one hand, it was a guaranteed ratings booster, a spectacle that would have listeners tuning in and talking for weeks. On the other hand, there was the slight chance of me, the host, plummeting to my doom live on air. But hey, what's life without a little risk, right?

As I ascended the platform, my heart pounded in my chest. I had never bungee jumped before, and the sight of the ground rushing up to meet me was more than a little unnerving. But I plastered a smile on my face, took a deep breath, and launched into my show.

"Welcome to 'The Ed Tyll Show,' broadcasting live from the edge of sanity!" I shouted into the microphone, my voice barely audible over the screams of bungee jumpers and the cheers of the crowd below.

The show was a chaotic blend of interviews, music, and, of

course, bungee jumping. I chatted with nervous jumpers as they waited their turn, their faces a mix of fear and exhilaration. I even interviewed a couple who had just gotten engaged on the platform, their leap of faith a perfect metaphor for their upcoming marriage.

But the real highlight of the day was when I decided to take the plunge myself. I strapped on the harness, my legs shaking uncontrollably, and stepped to the edge. The crowd below roared with encouragement, their cheers a mix of genuine support and morbid curiosity.

I took a deep breath, closed my eyes, and jumped.

The feeling was indescribable. It was a rush of pure adrenaline, a freefall into the unknown. I screamed, I laughed, I felt alive. And then, just as suddenly as it began, it was over. The bungee cord snapped me back up, and I was dangling upside down, my hair a mess, my clothes disheveled, but my spirit soaring.

The crowd erupted in applause, their cheers echoing through the air. I had faced my fear, conquered the bungee jump, and lived to tell the tale.

The rest of the day was a blur of bungee jumps, interviews, and laughter. I jumped with listeners, with my producers, and even with a few brave souls who had never bungee jumped before. It was a day of shared experiences, pushing boundaries and creating memories that would last a lifetime.

As the sun set over International Drive, I looked back on the day with a sense of accomplishment. I had not only hosted a successful radio show, but I had also conquered a personal fear and created a unique and unforgettable experience for my listeners.

And as I drove home that night, my body still buzzing with adrenaline, I knew this was just the beginning. The world was full of adventures waiting to be had, and I was ready to embrace them all, one bungee jump at a time.

Chapter 31

Snapping The First Pitch

The day started like any other for a seasoned talk radio host: a pre-dawn alarm, a strong cup of coffee, and the familiar buzz of the studio as I prepared for my morning show. But this wasn't just any day. Today, I was trading my microphone for a baseball, my studio for a helicopter, and my listeners for a stadium full of cheering fans.

You see, the local minor league baseball team had cooked up a wild promotional stunt: they wanted me, the city's most notorious radio personality, to arrive at the stadium in a news helicopter and throw out the first pitch. It was a crazy idea, but one that perfectly aligned with my penchant for the unexpected and the outrageous.

As I climbed into the helicopter, a mix of excitement and nerves coursed through me. I had never been in a helicopter before, let alone landed on a baseball field in front of thousands of people. But I was determined to make it memorable.

The pilot, a seasoned veteran with a mischievous grin, gave me a thumbs-up as we lifted off. The city sprawled out beneath us, a patchwork of buildings, streets, and palm trees bathed in the golden light of the morning sun.

As we approached the stadium, the crowd roared with anticipation. I could see the players warming up on the field, the grounds crew meticulously manicuring the diamond, and the mascot, a giant pelican with a mischievous glint in its eye, waving to the fans.

The pilot expertly maneuvered the helicopter towards the designated landing zone, the blades whirring loudly as we descended. The crowd's cheers grew louder, a deafening roar that drowned out even the sound of the engine.

With a gentle thud, the helicopter landed in the field. The pilot shut off the engine, and the crowd erupted in applause. I stepped out of the helicopter, my heart pounding in my chest, my hand clutching the baseball tightly.

I was escorted to the pitcher's mound, where the catcher, a burly man with a bushy mustache, was waiting for me. He gave me a reassuring nod, and I took my position.

I wound up, channeling my inner Nolan Ryan, and let the ball fly. It soared through the air, a perfect strike headed straight for the catcher's mitt. The crowd held its breath, the anticipation building.

With a satisfying snap, the ball landed in the catcher's glove. The crowd erupted in cheers, their voices echoing through the stadium. I had done it. I had thrown a strike, a perfect pitch that would be talked about for years to come.

As I walked off the field, the players and coaches congratulated me, their smiles genuine and their admiration evident. I had not only entertained the crowd, but I had also earned the team's respect.

The rest of the game was a blur of excitement, as the team battled their rivals in a nail-biting match. But the highlight of the day, for me and the fans, was that first pitch. It was a moment of pure magic, a testament to the power of spontaneity and the thrill of the unexpected.

And as I left the stadium that night, the cheers of the crowd still ringing in my ears, I knew that I had created a memory that would last a lifetime. It was a reminder that life is an adventure, and that sometimes, the most memorable moments are the ones that happen when you least expect them.

CHAPTER 32

DATING CRUISE

The sun glistened off the turquoise waters of the Caribbean as I boarded the luxurious cruise ship, embarking on a journey that promised romance, adventure, and a chance to find love on the high seas. This was no ordinary cruise; it was "The Ed Tyll Show Dating Cruise," a unique event I had created for my single listeners, offering them a chance to mingle, have fun, and potentially find their soulmate.

The ship was a haven for singles, buzzing with excitement and anticipation. The passengers were a diverse mix of personalities, all united by their desire for love and adventure. As the host of the show, I felt a responsibility to create an environment where everyone felt comfortable and had the opportunity to connect.

The cruise was packed with activities designed to foster romance and connection. There were speed dating sessions, cocktail parties, themed dance nights, and even a "love boat" scavenger hunt that sent couples on a playful adventure around the ship.

But the highlight of the cruise was undoubtedly the "Date with Ed" contest. I had offered to take one lucky listener out on a romantic date, and the competition was fierce. The entries poured in, filled with heartfelt stories, witty anecdotes, and declarations of love.

After careful consideration, I chose Emily, a charming and intelligent woman with a captivating smile and a twinkle in her eyes. We embarked on a whirlwind adventure, exploring the picturesque islands, indulging in delicious meals, and enjoying intimate conversations under the starlit sky.

Our date was a resounding success. We laughed, we talked, we shared stories, and we discovered a connection that went beyond the initial attraction. As we danced the night away under the disco ball, I realized that I had found something special in Emily.

The cruise ended too soon, but the memories we created would last a lifetime. We exchanged numbers, promised to stay in touch, and left the ship with a newfound hope for the future.

Back in the studio, the day after the cruise, I couldn't help but share my experience with my listeners. I recounted the laughter, the romance, and the unexpected connection I had found with Emily. My voice crackled with excitement as I spoke, the thrill of the experience still fresh in my mind.

The response was overwhelming. My listeners were captivated by my story, their imaginations sparked by the possibilities of finding love on the high seas. The cruise had been a success, not only for the couples who found each other, but also for the community of listeners who shared in the experience.

And as I looked out at the city from my studio window, the cityscape bathed in the warm glow of the setting sun, I knew that this was just the beginning. The Ed Tyll Show Dating Cruise had set sail, and its journey of love and adventure was far from over.

CHAPTER 33

NAKED BEACH RADIO SHOW

The phone lines lit up like a Christmas tree during my talk radio show, "The Ed Tyll Show," but the topic wasn't the usual mix of politics and pop culture. Instead, a passionate group of listeners was rallying to save a local treasure: Playalinda Beach, a clothing-optional haven nestled along Florida's Space Coast. A new, conservative county commissioner had vowed to shut it down, deeming it immoral and a blight on the community.

My listeners, a diverse group of free spirits, sun worshippers, and naturists, were outraged. They argued that Playalinda was a peaceful and secluded beach, enjoyed by families and individuals alike, and that closing it would be an infringement on their personal freedoms.

As the calls poured in, I realized that this was more than just a local issue. It was a battle for free speech, for the right to express oneself without fear of judgment or persecution. And as a free speech champion, I felt compelled to act.

On air, I announced my plan: I would broadcast my show live from Playalinda Beach, showcasing its natural beauty, its peaceful atmosphere, and the passionate community that cherished it. It was a bold move, a potential career-ender, but I was determined to stand up for what I believed in.

The day of the broadcast arrived. I packed my equipment into my trusty van, my heart pounding with a mix of excitement and apprehension. As I drove towards the beach, I couldn't help but wonder what I was getting myself into.

Arriving at Playalinda, I was greeted by a sea of smiling faces. My listeners had turned out in droves, their bodies painted with slogans like "Save Our Beach" and "Nudity is Natural." They had set up tents, grills, and even a makeshift stage for me to broadcast from.

As I stripped down to my birthday suit (hey, when in Rome...), I felt a sense of liberation. The sun on my skin, the sand between my toes, the sound of the waves crashing against the shore – it was a moment of pure bliss.

I took my place on the stage, adjusted my microphone, and launched into my show. The energy was electric, the atmosphere festive. I interviewed beachgoers, played music, and even led a group sing-along of "Born to Be Wild."

The broadcast was a resounding success. The phones rang off the hook, with callers from all over the country expressing their support for Playalinda and praising me for my courage in defending free speech. National news outlets picked up the story, and I became a symbol of the fight against censorship and prudery.

The county commissioner, however, was not amused. He denounced me as a "pervert" and a "public nuisance," vowing to shut down the beach regardless of the public outcry. But his threats fell on deaf ears. The people had spoken, and their message was clear: Playalinda Beach was here to stay.

In the end, the beach remained open, a testament to the power of community activism and the unwavering commitment to free speech. And I, the once-obscure radio host, had become a national figure, a champion of the First Amendment and a symbol of the fight against censorship.

The experience taught me a valuable lesson. Sometimes, the most important battles are fought not in courtrooms or legislatures, but on the beaches, in the streets, and on the airwaves. And as long as there are people willing to defend what they believe, the spirit of freedom will never be extinguished.

The broadcast from Playalinda Beach was a whirlwind, a blur of naked bodies, impassioned speeches, and the occasional rogue seagull swooping in for a closer look. But amidst the chaos, something extraordinary happened. The story of a talk radio host broadcasting live from a nude beach to protest its closure caught the attention of the national media.

First, it was the local news, with reporters flocking to the scene to capture the spectacle. Then, the story went national, with segments on CBS, ABC, NBC, and even CNN. Suddenly, I was no longer just a local radio personality; I was a symbol of free speech, a champion of the First Amendment, and a thorn in the side of conservative politicians.

The media attention was exhilarating and overwhelming. I was invited to appear on talk shows, interviewed by journalists from major newspapers, and even asked to give a keynote speech at a national convention for naturists.

The public reaction was equally intense. I received thousands of letters and emails, some praising me for my courage, others condemning me for my "indecency." My phone rang off the hook with interview requests, speaking engagements, and even a few marriage proposals (which I politely declined).

Overnight, I had become a household name, a polarizing figure who sparked both admiration and outrage. My show's ratings skyrocketed, and I was inundated with offers from other stations, networks, and even Hollywood producers.

But amidst the whirlwind of fame and notoriety, I remained grounded. I never forgot the reason I had broadcast from Playalinda Beach in the first place: to defend the rights of my listeners and to stand up for the principles of free speech.

I used my newfound platform to speak out on a variety of issues, from censorship and government overreach to social justice and environmental protection. I became a voice for the voiceless, a champion of the underdog, and a fearless critic of those in power.

Of course, not everyone was happy with my outspokenness. I received death threats, hate mail, and even a few protests outside my studio. But I refused to be silenced. I knew my voice mattered, and I was determined to use it to make a difference.

As the years passed, the initial frenzy died down, but my reputation as a fearless and outspoken broadcaster remained. I continued to host my show, tackle controversial topics, and push the boundaries of what was considered acceptable on the airwaves.

And while I never broadcast from a nude beach again (some experiences are best left as one-time events), I never forgot the lessons I learned that day. I learned that the power of the media can be a force for good, that speaking truth to power can have a real impact, and that even a humble radio host can make a difference in the world.

So, the next time you hear my voice on the radio, remember the story of the day I broadcast from Playalinda Beach. It's a story of courage, conviction, and the enduring power of free speech. And it's a reminder that sometimes, the most unexpected events can lead to the most extraordinary outcomes.

Chapter 34

#1 Ratings Day

The ratings came in like a tidal wave, washing away the old guard and ushering in a new era of talk radio. My show, "The Ed Tyll Show," had climbed to the top of the charts, unseating the long-reigning champion, a grumpy old-timer known for his predictable rants and outdated opinions. It was a David vs. Goliath victory, a triumph of fresh perspectives and innovative ideas over tired clichés and stale formats.

The news spread like wildfire through the industry. My name was on everyone's lips, my show the talk of the town. Advertisers, once hesitant to associate with my brand of irreverent humor, were now clamoring for a piece of the action. The station's sales team, previously accustomed to begging for scraps, was suddenly inundated with offers, their phones ringing off the hook with potential sponsors.

The station manager, a man who had once viewed me with skepticism, was now my biggest cheerleader. He praised my creativity, passion and ability to connect with listeners on a personal level. He even threw a celebratory party in my honor, complete with a custom-made cake shaped like a microphone.

But the real reward wasn't the fame, the money, or the accolades. It was the knowledge that I had made a difference, that I had changed the landscape of talk radio. I had proven that a show could be both entertaining and informative, that it could challenge listeners' assumptions and make them think, all while keeping them laughing.

My success also had a ripple effect on the industry. Other stations, seeing my show's popularity, began to take notice. They started to experiment with new formats, embrace diverse voices, and push the boundaries of what was considered acceptable on the airwaves. Talk radio was no longer just a platform for angry old men to rant about politics; it was a vibrant and dynamic medium that reflected the changing tastes and attitudes of the audience.

As for my old-fashioned competitor, he was forced to adapt or perish. He tried to inject some humor into his show, but his attempts fell flat. He tried to engage with callers on a more personal level, but his gruff demeanor and outdated opinions alienated listeners. In the end, he retired, grumbling about the "decline of civilization" and the "end of real talk radio."

With my competitor out of the picture, I became the undisputed king of talk radio. My show continued to dominate the ratings, attracting a loyal and passionate following. Advertisers flocked to the station, eager to reach my influential audience. The station's revenue soared, and its reputation as a leader in innovative programming was solidified.

And so, I had made my mark on the broadcast industry, not just as a successful talk radio host, but as a trailblazer who had helped to reshape the medium. My name became synonymous with cutting-edge radio, and my influence was felt far and wide.

But I never forgot my roots, the listeners who had supported me from the beginning. I continued to engage with them on air, to listen to their stories, and to champion their causes. I used my platform to give a voice to the voiceless, to challenge the status quo, and to make a difference in the world.

And as I looked back on my journey, from that first shaky

broadcast to the pinnacle of success, I couldn't help but feel a sense of gratitude. I had been given a gift, a voice that could reach millions. And I was determined to use that gift to entertain, inform and inspire.

National Syndication

CHAPTER 35

MOM PLEASE STEP OUT OF
THE CAR

Hosting a New Year's Eve gala was a dream for a talk radio host like me. The glitz, the glamor, the chance to rub elbows with the city's elite – it was all part of the allure. But when you add parents to the mix, things can take an unexpected turn.

My parents, bless their hearts, were not exactly party animals. My dad, a retired accountant, preferred a quiet evening at home with a good book and a glass of scotch. My mom, a former school-teacher, was more outgoing, but her idea of a wild night out was a game of bingo at the local church.

So, when I invited them to be my guests of honor at the New Year's Eve gala, I knew I was in for an interesting night.

The evening started off smoothly enough. My parents arrived looking dapper, my dad in a slightly ill-fitting tuxedo and my mom in a sparkly dress that she had bought for a cruise back in the '80s. They were clearly out of their element, but they were determined to make the most of it.

As the night wore on, the champagne flowed freely, the music got louder, and the dance floor filled with revelers. My parents, however, remained firmly planted at their table, sipping their drinks and observing the festivities with a mix of amusement and bemusement.

At one point, my mom, feeling a bit adventurous, decided to join me on the dance floor. We twirled and laughed, her infectious energy drawing a crowd of onlookers. But as the clock near midnight, my dad, ever the responsible one, decided it was time to call it a night.

We said our goodbyes to the other guests and headed out to the valet parking. As we waited for our car, my mom, feeling a bit tipsy from the champagne, started to sing "Auld Lang Syne" at the top of her lungs.

Suddenly, a police car pulled up, its lights flashing. The officer approached us, his face stern.

"Ma'am," he said, addressing my mom, "have you been drinking tonight?"

My mom, her face flushed with embarrassment, stammered, "Well, officer, I did have a few glasses of champagne."

The officer asked her to step out of the car and perform a field sobriety test. My dad and I watched nervously as my mom, her balance a bit wobbly, attempted to walk a straight line and touch her nose.

Minutes later, the officer returned, a smile on his face.

"Ma'am, you passed the test," he said. "But please be careful on your way home."

My mom, relieved and slightly embarrassed, thanked the officer and got back in the car. As we drove away, we all burst into laughter.

"Well, that was an adventure," my mom said, still giggling.

"I guess champagne and field sobriety tests aren't the best combination," my dad added, shaking his head.

I couldn't help but agree. It was a night we would never forget, a hilarious reminder that even the most glamorous events can take an unexpected turn when your parents are involved. But through it all, we had a great time, and we ended the night with a story that we would laugh about for years to come.

Chapter 36

Hollywood Hears

The Florida sun beat down on the palm-lined streets as I wrapped up another exhilarating episode of "The Ed Tyll Show." Little did I know that my voice, carried by the airwaves, was about to reach an unexpected audience thousands of miles away.

In a luxurious beachfront hotel suite in Los Angeles, two high-powered radio executives, Bob and Brenda, were enjoying a much-needed vacation. They had spent the day lounging by the pool, sipping margaritas, and brainstorming ideas for their struggling talk radio station back home.

As the sun began to set, casting a warm glow over the Pacific Ocean, Bob turned on the radio, hoping to catch some local news. Instead, he was greeted by a voice that was both familiar and refreshingly different. It was a voice filled with humor, wit, and a hint of mischief. It was my voice.

Bob, intrigued, called Brenda to listen. They sat there, captivated, as I launched into a hilarious rant about the absurdity of reality TV, followed by a thought-provoking discussion on the state of politics. My ability to seamlessly blend humor and intelligence, to entertain and inform, to connect with listeners on a personal level impressed them.

"Who is this guy?" Brenda asked, her eyes wide with curiosity.

Bob shrugged. "I don't know, but he's good. Really good."

They listened for the rest of the show, their laughter echoing through the suite as I shared anecdotes, interviewed guests, and fielded calls from listeners. By the end of the hour, they were convinced: they had found their next big star.

The next morning, Bob and Brenda were on the phone with their colleagues back in Los Angeles, raving about the unknown radio host they had discovered on their vacation. They instructed their team to track me down and extend an offer I couldn't refuse.

Days later, I received a call that would change my life. It was a talent scout from the Los Angeles station, offering me a lucrative contract to host their afternoon drive-time show. The offer included a generous salary, a spacious beachfront apartment, and the opportunity to work in the entertainment capital of the world.

I was stunned. Me? A small-town radio host from Florida, being offered a dream job in Los Angeles? It was almost too good to be true.

But it was true. After a whirlwind of negotiations and a tearful goodbye to my loyal Florida listeners, I packed my bags and headed west.

Moving to Los Angeles was seamless. The station welcomed me with open arms, the listeners embraced my unique brand of humor, and the city itself felt like home. I quickly became a fixture on the airwaves, my show a must-listen for Angelenos stuck in traffic on their way home from work.

My success in Los Angeles opened doors I had never dreamed of. I was invited to appear on national television shows, to host red-carpet events, and even to write a book about my experiences in the radio industry.

But through it all, I never forgot the fateful day when my voice reached the ears of two vacationing radio executives. It was a reminder that sometimes, the greatest opportunities come when you least expect them. And it was a testament to the power of radio, the ability to connect people across vast distances and create unexpected and life-changing moments.

The allure of Los Angeles, the city of dreams, fame, and endless sunshine, had always captivated me. As a seasoned talk radio host in Florida, I had carved out a comfortable niche for myself, entertaining listeners with my witty banter and offbeat humor. But when a call came from a prominent Los Angeles radio station, offering me a chance to join their lineup, I knew I was standing at the precipice of a potentially life-changing opportunity.

The station executives, sensing my hesitation in leaving the familiar comforts of Florida, decided to sweeten the deal. They flew me out to Los Angeles for a weekend of winning, dining, and a whirlwind tour of the city's most iconic landmarks.

My adventure began with a chauffeured drive down Rodeo Drive, the heart of Beverly Hills. As we cruised past designer boutiques, luxury car dealerships, and palm-lined streets dotted with sprawling mansions, I felt like I had stepped into a movie. The opulence and glamor were intoxicating, and I couldn't help but imagine myself living the life of a Hollywood insider.

Next, we ventured to Malibu, where I was treated to a breathtaking view of the Pacific Ocean from a cliffside restaurant. As I savored fresh seafood and sipped a glass of California wine, I couldn't help but feel a sense of awe. This was the life I had always dreamed of, the epitome of California cool.

But the real showstopper was visiting the Santa Monica Pier. As we strolled along the boardwalk, surrounded by street performers, amusement park rides, and the salty ocean breeze, I felt a surge of excitement. This was the Los Angeles I had always imagined, a vibrant and eclectic mix of cultures, lifestyles, and endless possibilities.

Over the weekend, station executives emphasized the perks of being a talk radio host in Los Angeles. They promised me access to exclusive events, celebrity interviews, and even a chance to walk the red carpet at movie premieres. They painted a picture of a life filled with excitement, opportunity, and endless sunshine.

By the end of the weekend, I was smitten. The city's energy, the station's vision, and the promise of a life beyond my wildest dreams were too tempting to resist. I accepted their offer, and within weeks, I was packing my bags and saying goodbye to Florida.

Moving to Los Angeles was seamless. The station welcomed me with open arms, the listeners embraced my humor and wit, and the city itself felt like a second home. I quickly became a fixture on the airwaves, my show a must-listen for Angelenos stuck in traffic on their way to work.

And the perks? Well, they were everything I had been promised and more. I attended star-studded events, interviewed A-list celebrities, and even walked the red carpet at a movie premiere (where I accidentally tripped and almost took down George Clooney).

But the real reward was the opportunity to live my dream, to be a part of the vibrant and exciting world of Los Angeles radio. And as I looked out at the city from my balcony, the Hollywood sign gleaming in the distance, I couldn't help but feel a sense of gratitude. I had been lured to Los Angeles by the promise of a better life, and I had found it in spades.

Los Angeles Fan Club

CHAPTER 37

A STODGE PODGE

The sprawling metropolis of Los Angeles, a city pulsating with ambition and dreams, was a far cry from the quiet suburbs where I had honed my talk radio skills. Fresh-faced and brimming with enthusiasm, I arrived at the station, my heart pounding with a mix of excitement and trepidation. This was it, the big leagues, where legends were made and careers were launched. But I soon discovered that the path to radio stardom was paved with more than just talent and ambition; it was also riddled with obstacles in the form of stodgy managers and jaded staff.

My first encounter with the old guard came during a pitch meeting with the program director, a man who looked like he had been weaned on a steady diet of cigarettes and cynicism. As I enthusiastically outlined my vision for a show that was fresh, innovative, and unapologetically irreverent, he stared at me with a blank expression, his eyes glazed over like donuts.

"Kid," he drawled, his voice dripping with condescension, "this is Los Angeles, not some backwater town where you can get away with that kind of nonsense. Our listeners expect sophistication, intelligence, and a certain level of decorum."

I tried to explain that my show was sophisticated, in its way. That it was intelligent, albeit with a healthy dose of humor. And that decorum, while important, didn't have to mean boring. But my words fell on deaf ears.

"Look," he said, cutting me off, "we've been doing this for years. We know what works and what doesn't. Just stick to the script, and you'll be fine."

The script, as it turned out, was a mind-numbingly dull collection of pre-approved topics, canned jokes, and generic interview questions. It was the antithesis of everything I believed in, a formulaic approach to radio that stifled creativity and originality.

But I was determined to make my mark. I started subtly injecting my own personality into the show, slipping in a witty remark here, a sarcastic comment there. I even dared to deviate from the script on occasion, exploring topics that were off-limits but undeniably interesting.

The listeners responded. My ratings slowly but steadily climbed, and I started to develop a loyal following. But the old guard was not amused. They accused me of being unprofessional, disrespectful, and a threat to the station's reputation.

One day, I was called into the station manager's office, a cavernous space filled with leather-bound books and framed photos of past radio legends. The station manager, a woman with a steely gaze and a reputation for being ruthless, sat behind a massive mahogany desk.

"Mr. Tyll," she said, her voice cold and authoritative, "we've been monitoring your show, and we're not happy with what we're hearing. You're not following the format, you're alienating our core audience, and you're making a mockery of this station."

I tried to defend myself, but she cut me off.

"We gave you a chance," she said, her voice rising with anger. "We thought you had potential. But you've proven to be nothing more than a reckless and irresponsible upstart. You're fired."

I was devastated. My dream of conquering Los Angeles radio had come crashing down around me. I felt like a failure, a fool who had dared to challenge the establishment and paid the price.

But as I walked out of the station, head held high, I realized that

I had no regrets. I had stayed true to myself, to my vision of what radio could be. And while I may not have won over the old guard, I had gained something far more valuable: the respect and admiration of my listeners.

And so, my journey as a talk radio host continued, albeit on a different path. I found a new station, one that embraced my unique style and encouraged my creativity. My show flourished, and I eventually became a popular voice in Los Angeles radio.

Looking back on that tumultuous time, I can't help but laugh. It was a baptism by fire, a trial by stodgy managers and jaded staff. But it was also a valuable lesson in perseverance, in the importance of staying true to oneself, and in the power of laughter to overcome even the most daunting obstacles.

CHAPTER 38

THE COOL GUYS STATION

Trapped in the clutches of a stuffy, old-fashioned talk radio station in Los Angeles, I felt like a caged bird, my wings clipped and my voice stifled. The station's rigid format, outdated playlists, and aversion to anything remotely controversial were a far cry from the dynamic and engaging radio I had envisioned.

My show, once a vibrant and unpredictable mix of humor, commentary, and audience interaction, had become a bland and formulaic affair. I was forced to stick to pre-approved topics, read scripted segments, and avoid any opinions that might offend the station's conservative, elderly demographic.

It was a soul-crushing experience, a slow death by a thousand paper cuts. My ratings plummeted, my creativity withered, and my once-passionate on-air persona became a hollow shell.

But just when I thought I was doomed to a lifetime of radio mediocrity, a savior appeared in the form of an old radio station manager named Max. Max, a seasoned industry veteran, had recently arrived in Los Angeles to take over a struggling competitor station. He was known for his innovative programming, his willingness to take risks, and his uncanny ability to spot untapped talent.

One day, while channel surfing through the Los Angeles airwaves, Max stumbled upon my show. He was immediately struck by the dissonance between my voice and the station's format. He heard the spark of creativity, the hint of rebellion, the potential for greatness that was being stifled by the station's outdated approach.

Max knew he had found his next big star.

He reached out to me, offering me a chance to join his station and create the kind of show I had always dreamed of. He promised me creative freedom, a supportive team, and a platform to reach a wider and more diverse audience.

I was hesitant at first. I had been burned before by promises of creative freedom that turned out to be empty. But Max was different. He had a proven track record of success, a genuine passion for radio, and a vision for the future that aligned with my own.

I accepted his offer, and within weeks, I was packing my bags and saying goodbye to the stuffy old station.

The transition was seamless. Max's station welcomed me with open arms, the staff eager to collaborate and the listeners hungry for something new and exciting. I was given free rein to develop my show, to experiment with different formats, and to tackle any topic that sparked my interest.

My show quickly became a hit, a refreshing and irreverent alternative to the stale and predictable offerings of other stations. I interviewed fascinating guests, debated controversial issues, and engaged in hilarious on-air antics. The listeners loved it, and the ratings soared.

Max was thrilled. He had taken a chance on me, and it had paid off in spades. He had rescued me from the clutches of radio mediocrity and given me the opportunity to shine.

And as I looked out at the city from my new studio window, the Hollywood sign gleaming in the distance, I couldn't help but feel a sense of gratitude. I had been given a second chance, a chance to do what I loved and make a difference in the talk radio world.

And it was all thanks to Max, the old radio station manager who had heard the spark of potential in my voice and gave me the opportunity to set it free.

The annual National Association of Broadcasters (NAB)

convention in Las Vegas was a whirlwind of activity, a sensory over-load of flashing lights, booming voices, and cutting-edge technol-ogy. Amidst the sea of suits and polished professionals, I stood out like a sore thumb, my brightly colored shirt and unruly hair a testa-ment to my unconventional approach to talk radio.

My show, known for its irreverent humor, provocative commentary, and occasional on-air antics, had gained a cult following in my local market. But I was hungry for more, eager to share my unique brand of radio with a wider audience.

As I navigated the crowded exhibit hall, my eyes were drawn to a booth adorned with sleek signage and a group of well-dressed execu-tives. It was the booth of a major national radio syndicator, a company that could make or break a broadcaster's career.

Nervously, I approached the booth, my heart pounding in my chest. I introduced myself to one of the executives, a tall, distin-guished-looking man with a piercing gaze.

"Ed Tyll," I said, extending my hand. "I'm a talk radio host from Florida, and I've been told you guys might be interested in my show."

The executive, his face a mask of professional politeness, nodded. "We're always on the lookout for fresh talent," he said. "Tell me about your show."

I launched into my pitch, describing my show's unique blend of humor, commentary, and audience interaction. I highlighted my ability to tackle controversial topics with a light touch, to make people laugh while also making them think.

The executive listened intently, his expression gradually shifting from polite interest to genuine amusement. He chuckled at my anecdotes, nodded approvingly at my insights, and even cracked a smile at my self-deprecating humor.

By the end of my pitch, he was hooked.

"You're a breath of fresh air in this industry," he said, his voice filled with enthusiasm. "Your show is exactly the kind of thing we're looking for. Let's talk."

We spent the rest of the convention discussing the details of a potential syndication deal. The executive was impressed by my passion, creativity and willingness to push the boundaries of traditional talk radio.

A few weeks later, I received the call I had been waiting for. The syndication deal was finalized, and my show was going national.

The news spread like wildfire through the industry. My name was on everyone's lips, my show the talk of the town. Advertisers, once hesitant to associate with my brand of irreverent humor, were now clamoring for a piece of the action.

My show's success was a testament to the power of personality-driven radio. In a world of pre-packaged content and cookie-cutter formats, my show stood out as a unique and authentic voice. It was a reminder that radio, at its best, is a conversation, a connection between a host and their listeners.

And as I looked out at the vast expanse of the country from my studio window, I couldn't help but feel a sense of awe. My voice, once confined to a small corner of Florida, was now reaching millions of people across the nation.

It was a dream come true, a testament to the power of perseverance, creativity and a little luck. And it all started with a chance encounter at a crowded convention booth in Las Vegas.

The sun-drenched oasis of my newly furnished Los Angeles home was a testament to my hard-earned success. Plush leather sofas, a state-of-the-art entertainment system, and a panoramic view of the city skyline were the spoils of my burgeoning talk radio career. Life was good, comfortable even. But as they say, you can't rest on your laurels in the cutthroat world of broadcasting.

Just as I was settling into my luxurious new digs, my syndicator dropped a bombshell. They had expanded the network, adding more stations across the country, and wanted me to spearhead the expansion by relocating to a brand new, state-of-the-art studio. The catch? The studio was in Chicago. Chicago, the windy city, the land of deep-dish pizza and bone-chilling winters.

I was torn. On one hand, this was a massive opportunity, a chance to take my career to the next level and reach a wider audience. On the other hand, it meant leaving behind the sunny skies and laid-back lifestyle of Los Angeles for a city where the temperature regularly dipped below freezing.

After much deliberation, I decided to take the plunge. I packed my bags, bid farewell to my beloved palm trees, and boarded a plane bound for the Windy City. As the plane descended, I caught my first glimpse of the snow-covered landscape, a stark contrast to the sun-kissed beaches I had left behind.

The new studio was everything I had imagined and more. It was a technological marvel, equipped with the latest broadcasting equipment, soundproof booths, and a spacious control room that looked like something out of a sci-fi movie. But as I stepped outside for a lunch break, the frigid wind slapped me in the face like an angry polar bear.

I quickly realized that life in Chicago was going to be a whole different ball game. I had to invest in a heavy-duty winter coat, learn to navigate the city's notoriously confusing grid system, and develop a taste for deep-dish pizza (which, I must admit, was surprisingly delicious).

But the biggest challenge was adapting my on-air persona to a new audience. The Chicago listeners were a tough crowd, their humor drier, their opinions more outspoken, and their expectations higher. I had to up my game, sharpen my wit, and find new ways to connect with them.

Slowly but surely, I started to win them over. My ratings climbed, the feedback was positive, and I even started to develop a loyal following. I discovered that Chicagoans, despite their tough exterior, had a warmth and a sense of humor that rivaled any city I had ever lived in.

And so, I embraced my new home, the challenges and the rewards that came with it. I learned to appreciate the beauty of a snow-covered skyline, the camaraderie of a shared winter experience, and the thrill of conquering a new frontier.

And while I still missed the sunshine and palm trees of Los Angeles, I knew that I had made the right decision. I had taken a leap of faith, stepped outside my comfort zone, and landed on my feet in a city that was both challenging and rewarding.

And as for my career? Well, let's just say moving to Chicago was the best decision I ever made. My show became a national sensation, my name synonymous with cutting-edge talk radio. And while I may have traded the sunshine for the snow, I gained something far more valuable: the opportunity to grow, to evolve, and to make my mark on the world of broadcasting.

Detroit Fans

CHAPTER 39

NEW YORK CITY CHANGES

BEFORE MY EYES

The hallowed halls of WABC Radio, the undisputed king of talk radio in New York City, were a testament to broadcasting history. Growing up, my family had gathered around the radio, their ears tuned to the voices that shaped the city's discourse. It was the station that had sparked my passion for radio, the dream I had chased since my first awkward broadcast in high school. And now, here I was, standing in the very studio where legends had made their mark, auditioning for the coveted afternoon drive-time slot.

The audition was a blur of nerves and adrenaline. I stumbled through my opening monologue, my voice cracking under the weight of expectation. But as I warmed up, my passion took over. I riffed on current events, shared personal anecdotes, and engaged in lively banter with the producers. By the end of the hour, I felt a sense of accomplishment, a glimmer of hope that I had made a good impression.

As I left the studio, the city that never sleeps was buzzing with its usual energy. People rushed down crowded sidewalks, yellow taxis honked impatiently, and the towering skyscrapers cast long shadows over the bustling streets. But a sense of unease hung in the air, a feeling that something was not quite right.

The next morning, the world changed forever. The catastrophic attack on the World Trade Center sent shockwaves through the city, the country, and the entire world. The once-invincible skyline was forever altered, a gaping hole where the Twin Towers had once stood.

In the aftermath of the tragedy, the city was gripped by fear, grief, and uncertainty. The radio station, a pillar of strength and resilience, became a lifeline for New Yorkers seeking information, comfort, and a sense of community. But the attack also had a profound impact on the station itself.

The once-booming advertising market dried up, the station's financial stability was shaken, and its future was uncertain. The management, faced with difficult decisions, decided to sell the station to a new owner with a different vision for its programming.

My dream of hosting a show was shattered. The station I had grown up listening to, the station that had inspired my career, was no longer the same. It was a heartbreaking loss, a reminder of the fragility of even the most iconic institutions.

But amidst the disappointment, a new opportunity emerged. A small, independent station in the suburbs, looking to capitalize on the changing media landscape, offered me a chance to host my own show. It was a chance to keep my dream alive.

I accepted the offer, and within weeks, I was on the air, broadcasting from a cramped studio in a strip mall. The audience was smaller, the resources were limited, but the freedom was exhilarating. I could tackle any topic, express any opinion, and experiment with new formats without fear of censorship or reprisal.

My show quickly gained a loyal following, attracted by my honest and unfiltered commentary, my willingness to tackle controversial issues, and my ability to find humor even in the darkest of times. The station's ratings climbed, advertisers took notice, and my career was back on track.

And while I never forgot the dream of hosting a show on WABC, I realized that my journey had taken me on a different, but equally rewarding path. I had found my voice, my audience, and my place in the ever-evolving world of talk radio.

And as I looked out at the city from my suburban studio window, the skyline forever changed. But the New York spirit was still strong, I knew I had landed on my feet. I had survived the storm, adapted to the changing landscape, and emerged stronger and more resilient than ever before.

Hometown Host

CHAPTER 40

GREENWICH VILLAGE COMEDIAN

The suburban talk radio station had been a comfortable gig, a steady paycheck and a loyal audience. But deep down, I yearned for something more, a creative outlet that would allow me to push boundaries and explore the depths of my comedic potential. Stand-up comedy, with its raw energy and unfiltered expression, had always beckoned me, a siren song promising both exhilaration and terror.

When the station offered me a generous contract buyout, it was the push I needed to take the leap. With a newfound financial freedom and a burning desire to prove myself, I set my sights on the legendary comedy clubs of Greenwich Village, the birthplace of countless comedic legends.

My first few performances were a mix of exhilaration and abject terror. The bright lights, the expectant audience, the unforgiving microphone – it was a baptism by fire. My jokes, carefully crafted and honed over countless hours, sometimes landed with a thud, met with awkward silence or polite chuckles. But other times, they struck a chord, eliciting roars of laughter and applause.

As I honed my craft, I began to develop a unique comedic voice, a blend of observational humor, social commentary, and self-deprecating wit. I wasn't afraid to tackle controversial topics, to challenge the audience's assumptions, and to push the boundaries of good taste.

Word of my edgy and liberating comedy spread quickly through the Village. I started to attract a following, a group of like-minded individuals who appreciated my willingness to speak truth to power and to find humor in the absurdity of life.

One night, after a particularly successful set, a group of fellow comedians who had been watching from the back of the room approached me. My performance, my fearlessness, and my unique perspective impressed them.

"You're a breath of fresh air in this stale scene," one of them said, a lanky guy with a mop of curly hair and a mischievous grin.

"We're tired of the same old jokes, the same old routines," another added, a woman with a sharp wit and a piercing gaze.

"We want to create something new, something different, something that challenges the status quo," a third chimed in, a bearded man with a booming voice and a rebellious spirit.

We started meeting regularly, brainstorming ideas, writing jokes, and honing our individual comedic styles. We formed a collective, a group of misfits and outsiders who were united by our passion for comedy and our desire to push the boundaries of what was considered acceptable.

We called ourselves "The Mad Boys," a nod to our rebellious spirit and our refusal to conform to the mainstream. We performed at small clubs, underground venues, and even on the streets of the Village, our shows a mix of stand-up, sketch comedy, and performance art.

Our shows were raw, unfiltered, and often controversial. We tackled taboo subjects, mocked authority figures, and challenged the audience's preconceived notions. We were not afraid to offend, provoke or make people uncomfortable.

But we were also funny. Hilarious, even. Our jokes were sharp, our timing impeccable, and our energy infectious. We had a knack for finding humor in the darkest of places, for turning pain into laughter, and for making people think while they were laughing.

The Mad Boys quickly became a sensation, our shows drawing crowds of loyal fans and curious onlookers. We were featured in newspapers, magazines, and even on television, our reputation as the most edgy and liberating comedy group in the city growing with each performance.

And while our success was gratifying, it was never our primary goal. We were driven by a passion for comedy, a desire to express ourselves freely, and a belief in the power of laughter to challenge, to inspire, and to change the world.

And so, The Mad Boys continued to perform, to push boundaries, and to make people laugh. We were a force to be reckoned with, a testament to the power of creativity, collaboration, and the unwavering belief in the transformative power of comedy.

My place on the Greenwich Village comedy scene was a whirlwind of laughter, adrenaline, and a healthy dose of self-deprecating humor. From the humble beginnings of my suburban talk radio gig to the electrifying energy of MacDougal Street, my journey was a testament to the power of perseverance, creativity, and the occasional well-timed joke.

The Mad Boys, the group I had formed with my fellow misfits, had become a force to be reckoned with. Our shows were packed with eager audiences, our reputation grew, and our comedic influence spread beyond the confines of the Village.

One fateful night, we were performing at a legendary comedy club on MacDougal Street, the heart and soul of the Village's vibrant comedy scene. The club owner, a grizzled veteran with a keen eye for talent, was in the audience that night.

As I took the stage, a wave of nervous energy washed over me. The spotlight glared down, the crowd's expectant faces filled the room, and the weight of expectation settled heavily on my shoulders. But as I launched into my set, the nerves melted away, replaced by the familiar rush of adrenaline and the infectious energy of the audience.

My jokes landed perfectly, the laughter echoing through the room like a symphony of approval. I riffed on current events, poked fun at pop culture, and even took a few jabs at the club owner himself, who chuckled good-naturedly from his seat in the back.

By the end of my set, the crowd was roaring with laughter, their applause thunderous. The club owner approached me, his face beaming with a smile.

"You're a natural," he said, his voice gruff but genuine. "I'd like to offer you a six-night-a-week hosting gig at the club."

I was ecstatic. This was the opportunity I had been waiting for, a chance to perform on the most iconic stage in the Village, to share my comedic voice with a wider audience, and to establish myself as a force to be reckoned with in the world of stand-up comedy.

The next few months were a blur of activity. I honed my material, perfected my timing, and developed a rapport with the diverse crowds that flocked to the club. My six-night-a-week hosting gig became a training ground, a crucible where I learned to adapt my comedy to different audiences, to handle hecklers with grace, and to deliver a consistently hilarious performance even when I was exhausted.

My success on MacDougal Street attracted media attention. Newspapers and magazines featured articles about me, radio shows interviewed me, and even a documentary filmmaker approached me to make a film about my life and career.

The documentary, titled "The Mad Boys," chronicled my journey from the suburbs to the Village, from talk radio to stand-up, from obscurity to fame. It captured the raw energy of my performances, the camaraderie of my fellow Outlaws, and the transformative power of comedy.

The film was a critical and commercial success, further solidifying my position in the world of stand-up comedy. I was no longer just a local comedian; I was a sensation, a voice for the disaffected, and a champion of the absurd.

But through it all, I never forgot my roots, my fellow Mad Boys, and the small bar on MacDougal Street that had given me my first big break. I continued to perform there, to connect with my audience, and to push the boundaries of comedy with every joke, every performance, every laugh.

And as I looked out at the crowd, their faces illuminated by the stage lights, their laughter echoing through the room, I knew that I had found my place, my voice, and my purpose. I was a comedian, a provocateur, a storyteller, and an outlaw, forever bound to the vibrant and ever-evolving world of stand-up comedy.

MC Ed Tyll

THE END

Afterword

I wanted to share these stories from my radio career not just for laughs, but also to share my passion for this wild and unpredictable industry. Talk radio, with all its ups and downs, has been an incredible journey for me. It's allowed me to connect with people from all walks of life, to share my thoughts and ideas with a wide audience, and to make a difference in the communities I've served.

But more than that, I believe my story is a testament to the power of following your dreams, no matter how crazy or unconventional they may seem. I started as a boy with a big voice and an even bigger ambition. Through hard work, perseverance, and a healthy dose of humor, I was able to turn my passion into a successful career.

So if you have a dream, whether it's in radio, writing, or any other field, don't be afraid to chase it. Embrace the challenges, learn from your mistakes, and never give up on yourself. And who knows, maybe one day you'll be writing your own afterword, sharing your own incredible journey with the world.

Ed Tyll